CONVERSATIONS IN A SMALL COUNTRY
Scottish Interviews

"He's interviewed a number of well-known people — including me — but they're not the usual whitewash interviews. They're really very searching pieces, very revealing. In my own interview, I was certainly startled by what I'd revealed!" – *Rikki Fulton, The Scotsman.*

"A revealing portrait of the nation." – *Scotland on Sunday.*

"Kenneth Roy's skill can be eerie . . . For readers there is the thrill of eavesdropping. The conversations have the joy of listening on a crossed phone line." – *William Hunter, Glasgow Herald.*

"All the interviews are fascinating." – *Kenyon Wright, The Scotsman.*

"Kenneth Roy's name and broadcasting expertise are well appreciated . . . He has used his professional skills to record fascinating aspects of the lives and attitudes of 23 famous Scots." –*Stornoway Gazette.*

"This is a book by a very fine journalist . . . I've kept it by the side of the bed!" – *Margo MacDonald, Scottish Books (STV).*

Also by Kenneth Roy

Travels in a Small Country

CONVERSATIONS IN A SMALL COUNTRY
Scottish Interviews

by

Kenneth Roy

CARRICK PUBLISHING
Ayr

To Stephen and Christopher Roy

First published in 1989 by
Carrick Publishing
28 Miller Road, Ayr KA7 2AY
Telephone 0292 266679

Set by Communitype, Leicester
Printed in Great Britain by Billing & Sons Ltd., Worcester

British Library Cataloguing in Publication Data

Roy, Kenneth   *1945* -

  Conversations in a small country: Scottish interviews
  1.   Scotland.   Social life, 1901--Biographies - Collections
  I.   Title
  941.1082'092'2
ISBN 0-946724-22-9

Second Impression 1990

CONTENTS

PREFACE

Two years ago, in the weeks leading up to and immediately after the 1987 general election, I went on a journey through Scotland. An account of the journey was subsequently published in a book called Travels in a Small Country.

In the preface, I wrote: "About five million at the last count inhabit this small space on the edge of Europe; they include a number of stray English and other exotic species, but most of the space is occupied by us, the indigenous variety. Who are we, what do we think, how do we behave? I am not sure. It was a curiosity to find the answers which sent me on my journey."

In the event, what I found was not very encouraging — the book adopted a generally dark view of Scotland and the Scots. When the Glasgow Herald published several long extracts, the correspondence columns quickly filled with vituperative letters from places as far apart as Tobermory and Bannockburn. One reader of the newspaper more or less challenged me to a duel outside his pub, an invitation that I had no difficulty in declining.

It occurred to me then that I might have got it badly wrong. The portrait of my fellow countrymen was always going to be partial and prejudiced — the book did not set out to be fair — but the ferocity of the reaction surprised me. I decided upon a sequel which would give a variety of other Scots an opportunity to reveal something of themselves and their opinions, keeping myself out of it as far as possible but addressing basically the same questions as the earlier book. Conversations in a Small Country is that sequel.

September 1989   K.R.

Stormy Petrel

TAM DALYELL

"All those old Etonians, many of whom are friends of mine, have been absolutely gutless in dealing with the woman."

"Why?"

"Because they've never had to argue with a woman about other than personal or family matters. She should be stuck up to, and confronted. Bloody well treated like a man."

Tam Dalyell, possibly the only old Etonian in history who has been thrown out of the House of Commons five times for accusing a Prime Minister of lying, was telling me why the public school system is to blame for what he sees as the break-up of Cabinet government in Britain in the last 10 years.

Once upon a time — I have Mr Dalyell's word for this — he and Mrs Thatcher got on perfectly civilly. He said she was one of the few Tories to whom his former boss, Dick Crossman, would bid good morning. So might it be possible, even now, to persuade him to say something nice about the Prime Minister?

We were sitting on the terrace of the House of Commons on a grey June morning. On the far side of the river, a boat carrying the latest paunch of American tourists tooted its horn to acknowledge the Mother of Parliaments. A bitter wind whistled down the terrace, whipping away papers and rattling coffee cups.

"Is there anything about her I admire?" he repeated.

"I'm trying to wring a compliment out of you."

"I have to admire," he said bleakly, "a certain gut courage after the Brighton bomb. I also wished her well as the first woman Prime

Minister." Pause. "But I cannot forgive her for what she did during the miners' strike. What she did, not to heal the situation in the coalfield, but to make it worse. Macmillan was a healer, Alec Home was a healer, even Heath was a healer. But not this bloody woman."

Tam Dalyell has a wonderfully brooding and unpredictable presence. One never knows quite what he is going to say next, or how he is going to say it, or sometimes even why. In the days before television, he would have made a barnstorming actor-manager, shocking and delighting the provinces with his full-blooded rendering of Victorian melodramas and cliff-hanging thrillers. Instead he has been treading the boards at Westminster for the last quarter of a century, a one-man show of undiminished bravura in the midst of so much dreary ensemble playing.

Having disposed of Mrs Thatcher, I thought we should get rid of Mr Kinnock, too.

"He seems to be moving steadily right. Is that the fate of all Labour leaders?"

Mr Dalyell's reply said nothing at all about Mr Kinnock. The wily old performer heard the cue, but chose to deliver a different speech.

"I think you've got to be very clear about these terms right and left. I mean, what am I? One of the most vehement members of the Parliamentary Labour Party for getting the Army out of Northern Ireland, and therefore on the far left. On the other hand, an unreconstructed, constant pro-European Community man, which puts me on the extreme right. And where does my strong support for the nuclear industry put me? On the right, I suppose. But I am also shoulder to shoulder with the left in favour of a wealth tax. This categorisation is very difficult."

Tam Dalyell, who fits no known pigeon hole, has been a master of surprise ever since his student days, when as chairman of Cambridge University Conservative Association he decided he was in the wrong party.

"How did you end up a socialist? Was it a gradual conversion?"

"It certainly wasn't Paul on the road to Damascus!" Mr Dalyell laughed, as he often did during our conversation. He uses laughter as a weapon, usually in self-defence.

"I had a lot of left-wing friends. We used to go to each other's meetings. But the truth is, I was an intervener by nature. The other thing was that I'd probably seen a side of life that a number of my contemporaries from a similar background hadn't, in that I'd been a trooper in the Scots Greys tank crew during my national service. And if one becomes a trooper in a regiment which one's ancestor has founded, and everyone bloody well knows it, one is either broken or one becomes unembarrassable. I'm very unembarrassable!"

"About everything?"

"Other than trivial things. I'm sometimes embarrassed about my relations with people if I feel that I've done them a wrong."

"But that's all?"

"Yuh. Great strength, actually!"

His soldier ancestor was also a Tam: General Tam, who defeated the covenanters at Rullion Green and raised the Royal Scots Greys at the Binns, historic home of the Dalyell family. The present Tam took the salute when the regiment paraded there for the last time in 1971.

"What do you remember of your mother and father?"

"I was the only child of relatively elderly parents. My mother was indefatigable. An extremely intelligent woman, a doer of good works. My father came from an interesting family. He was one of those absolutely incorruptible Edwardian Anglo-Indian civil servants, who had followed his father, grandfather and great-grandfather into the Indian political service. Albeit old-fashioned, a man of considerable probity."

And, it seems, of some chivalry. His name was Gordon Loch. In 1928, he married Eleanor Dalyell. Nine years later, on her father's death, the couple inherited the Binns. In the interests of historical continuity — there had been Dalyells at the Binns for more than 300 years — Mr Loch gave up his own name and took his wife's. Had it not been for this decision, one of our greatest back-bench MPs would have been known as Tam Loch, a name more socialist in resonance, perhaps, but belonging more naturally to some bearded singer of revolutionary Scottish folk-songs.

"Do you think your father would have approved of your becoming a Labour politician?"

"He was very unpolitical. Definitely not a fan of Baldwin, nor of Churchill."

"What was his ambition for you?"

"He just said gently that he thought the family had had enough of

India, that India wasn't going to last in the way that it had for generations, and that he didn't want me to become an Indian civil servant. He took the view that I really had to make up my own mind, but that he would give me the best education that he could."

"So you were sent to Eton. How did you get on there?"

"Very well, and I've kept up with them. I was for a long time the only old Etonian Labour MP."

"Do I take it that you're in favour of retaining private education?"

"Ah, you mustn't jump to that conclusion. I think Eton has great merits and if you want pro consuls to run Nigeria, Ghana and heaven knows where, on the whole I think old Etonians are quite good at it. For the modern world, I'm not so sure. My own son and daughter went to Queensferry High School. They are, so far as I can tell, happy, balanced, rounded children, who've done well at university."

So I put the question the other way round. Was he for abolishing private education?

"Am I in favour of...." (laughs) "...Henry McLeish's statement..." (laughs) "on the front page of the Scotsman?" As Big Ben tolled 10, the sudden gust of laughter threatened to become a whirlwind. "I think I'd talk to Nigel Griffiths and Alistair Darling about that! I don't go losing my colleagues their constituencies!"

He was still laughing on the tenth bong. What on earth was he on about?

Later, I discovered that Mr McLeish, the Labour MP for Central Fife, had said something indiscreet about private education which might prove electorally unpopular in the marginal Edinburgh constituencies of Mr Griffiths and Mr Darling.

My search for Tam Dalyell continued.

"You became a history teacher at Bo'ness Academy. Were you a good teacher?"

"Yes, in my opinion, and in the opinion of many of those, 25 years later, who are my constituents. I might add, a very good teacher indeed for a lot of pupils. Why? Because I took a lot of trouble over them. I was very formal with them in class, but outside, I did all sorts of things. For example, I helped run the school football team. In fact, I became an MP through football."

"Oh, really? Tell me how."

But he craftily let his wonderful line hang in the air, pretended not to hear my question, and went on to tell me that he had also run the school chess club; which in turn prompted an extended anecdote about a recent visit to the House of Commons by the chess master, Kasparov.

"I was one of the 21 who took on Mr Kasparov. Raymond Keene, the chess correspondent of the Times, said the most flattering thing that's ever been said to me. He said my game was so interesting that he was going to publish it in the paper. And he did, three Saturdays ago. Dalyell White versus Kasparov Black."

"How did it go?"

"Kasparov played rook's pawn to rook five, and then to rook six, for which I would have criticised any of my Bo'ness pupils. But then he pinned me down in a piece of brilliant play — there was absolutely nothing I could do about it. As Raymond Keene put it, that's why he's world champion and you're not!" Mr Dalyell let out another great bellow of a laugh. "I had dinner with Kasparov afterwards. Fascinating man."

"Could we get back to the football?"

We did eventually, via an account of his first Parliamentary candidature in Roxburgh, Selkirk and Peebles ("against a nice, civilised Tory") and some random reflections on Parliamentary manners ("my own are impeccable").

About the football. Mr Dalyell's running of the Bo'ness Academy team was so successful that the grandfather of one of the boys ("a very difficult youth") decided that the manager should be rewarded for services to his grandson. "He gave me that which he had in his keeping, namely the nomination of his trade union, NACODS, when my predecessor as MP for West Lothian died suddenly. The late Abe Moffat (Scottish miners' leader) did his nut. He had wanted the seat for somebody else."

Thus the young man from the big house, with the top-drawer accent and Eton education, emerged as one of the unlikelier standard-bearers of the Scottish working-class.

"Who was your main opponent?"

"Billy Wolfe of the SNP. We were to fight seven times. I think we're in the Guinness Book of Records."

"Were you as opposed to Scottish nationalism before you stood for Parliament as you are now?"

"I think you've got to get me right on this. Unlike most of my colleagues, I have never in any way abused the nationalists. I have always taken them extremely seriously, and with total courtesy. Look, there are two options. Either we are fully part of the British state OR a separate state. What I don't believe in is half-way houses."

Tam Dalyell's dislike of half-way houses inspired one of the great campaigns of his career. In the devolution debate of the late Seventies, he was tenacious in exploiting a serious flaw in his party's plans for a Scottish Assembly: that while, when the Assembly came, the same number of Scottish MPs at Westminster would continue to be able to exert influence on English legislation, English MPs would be denied an equivalent say in Scottish matters. How, he asked, could this be justified? At every conceivable opportunity, on every available platform, he asked this awkward question. He went on and on asking it, wearing down resistance, exhausting all around him, until finally the question itself entered the Parliamentary vocabulary. It became known as the West Lothian Question.

"Do you think your own contribution to the devolution debate was a significant factor in the eventual outcome?"

"Yes, because if one Scot hadn't opposed it, the others wouldn't have felt they could have played their part, and the whole thing would have gone through. Jim Callaghan privately agreed with me. When I went to see him, he used to say, 'Don't waste my time on that nonsense. Tell me what the party's thinking about Cyprus.'"

James Callaghan is one of five Prime Ministers who have come and gone during Tam Dalyell's Parliamentary career. Despite his best efforts, the sixth is proving obstinately durable, but even she may be seen off in the end.

"I'm one of the dwindling band who remembers Macmillan. Macmillan was very kind to me. Of course those were the days when there was civilised debate. After about five or six months here, I asked a question. Would the Prime Minister ensure that legislation presented to the House was not drafted in obscure language? Macmillan's reply was quite brilliant. He replied — Look, I'll get the reply for you from the library, if you like."

As Mr Dalyell left to go hunting for a 27-year-old excerpt from Hansard, the young nationalist MP, Alex Salmond, arrived with two visitors. When he returned a few minutes later, Mr Salmond and his guests were still on the terrace taking photographs. Mr Dalyell kindly offered to act as cameraman for a group picture, and for a moment, there was the affecting spectacle of a smiling Mr Salmond posing for the well-known Nat-basher's happy snaps.

"You were talking about the days of civilised debate. Are they not civilised now?"

"Well, they're not civilised with this Prime Minister and this Secretary of State for Scotland, because they both systematically want to denigrate the opposition. Whenever there was a problem in the past, I had no hesitation in going to George Younger, Gordon Campbell, Michael Noble or that sweet, nice man, Jack Maclay. Things today are totally different. Malcolm Rifkind talks about having a Gatling gun. I don't think that people with 10 out of 72 MPs should talk about having a Gatling gun. In fact, it's an occasion for them to be even more emollient and helpful than their predecessors."

The bad blood between Tam Dalyell and Malcolm Rifkind had its origins in the notorious Special Branch raid on the BBC's Glasgow studios. "Rifkind said he didn't know there was going to be a raid until the Saturday. He knew damn well on the Tuesday. Because I called him a liar, he said he wouldn't talk to me. It's gone on now for two years and two months."

"You haven't exchanged a word?"

"No. Other than across the floor of the House of Commons. And Thatcher has done the same thing. Told a self-preserving lie to the House of Commons. On January 27, 1986."

But I had heard enough for one morning about Mrs Thatcher and her legendary powers of self-preservation. Instead, I asked him for an opinion of the other Prime Ministers he had known.

"Harold Wilson I knew extremely well. I was sad that Wilson never gave me a job in his government. Maybe that was more my fault than his, because I'd got into such great trouble over a number of campaigns and the Privileges Committee were out to get me. Maybe a campaigner like me cannot expect to be given ministerial office, pursuing so ferociously the campaigns that I did. I was a very stormy petrel indeed."

"If you had become a minister, what job would you have liked?"

"It may sound very strange, but the ministerial job that I would really have liked, and probably now it is impossible because of party policy, was Secretary of State for Northern Ireland with a remit to get the British Army out."

"You made a tremendous fuss over the Falklands. Did you receive a lot of hate mail about that?"

"Hate mail, human excrement, bad fish, white feathers." That laugh again. Then, seriously: "But only two complaints from my own constituency."

"Why did you get so worked up?"

"Because I thought the Task Force was in great danger, I thought it was foolhardy. You see, one of the complex things about me is that I'm very serious about the forces."

"You were proved wrong, though."

"In what?"

"Well, the expedition didn't prove to be foolhardy."

"They were extremely brave, and bloody lucky — because had the bombs been properly primed, our ships Glasgow and Plymouth would have gone up. Where I was right was that relations with Argentina still haven't been mended."

After an hour with Tam Dalyell, I was still smarting from my abject defeat on the question of private education. So I tried again from a different angle.

"Tony Crosland once defined socialism this way: 'Until we are truly equal, we will not be truly free.' Do you go along with that?"

"Tony Crosland's book, The Future of Socialism, was a great influence. But no, I don't go along with it. Equality of wealth, equality of education...these are rather unreal ideals, aren't they?"

"Socialist ideals?"

"They are things to which one should strive."

"Socialist ideals?"

"They are very stark. What do you mean by equality? I mean, equality of education depends a great deal on luck. Whether you have good or bad teachers. I was extremely lucky. I was superbly taught."

"Is a social hierarchy inevitable?"

"No. I hope that in my own life, I follow the old Scots tradition of treating everybody as I find them, whoever they are. Courtesy and respect to all."

I wondered how much courtesy and respect he would extend, when pressed, to his own leader.

"Mr Kinnock. Is he doing a good job for the party?"

There was a longish pause, and Mr Dalyell chose his words with some care. "I think generally if he got a chance to be Prime Minister, he'd make a good Prime Minister. I think he is as nice as ever, and as talkable-to as ever. And he's putting his questions more succinctly. And I propose to back him."

It was not the most glowing endorsement of a party leader I had ever heard.

"Is there anything in your life that's more important to you than politics?"

"My wife, who is very politically interested, says I'm too obsessed by politics. My family means a helluva lot to me. I'm extremely fortunate in that for 27 years, I've been married to a remarkable woman." (Kathleen, daughter of the late Scottish judge, Lord Wheatley.)

"How important is religion to you?"

"In a general sense, very important. I'm ecumenical. I was brilliantly taught. I am theologically serious."

"When you say you're ecumenical, what does that mean?"

"It means I believe in God."

"Do you think a lot about God?"

He shifted uneasily in his chair. "I think a lot about ethics," he said quietly. "You know. Things are either right or wrong."

"Not quite the same thing as God."

"Look, what are you asking me to say? That I'm a holy man?" And he resorted once more to laughter.

"It was a reasonable question."

Silence.

"To which I reply that I believe in God, and am deeply concerned with Christian ethics. If you ask me whether I am a Holy Willie: no. Am I interested in cathedral architecture? Passionately. Am I interested in the history of religions? Yes. Am I interested in other people's religions? Very."

"Are you ecumenical in the sense that you would like to see the churches more united?"

"Yes."

"How united?"

Not for the first time, I received an oblique answer. "I was appalled," he said, "at the treatment of Lord Mackay for going to my father-in-law's requiem mass, and I knew that there would be trouble as soon as I saw him there. It was very good of him to come."

"When were you happiest?"

The old campaigner gazed out at the river. "I'm always happy," he said slowly. "I'm a very happy man. I've never been unhappy. But I've been very lucky. I sometimes have a gloomy expression, and I suppose I often get very tired. But happy. Always happy."

"Well, that's a good way to end."

Uproarious laughter.

We trudged upstairs to the library to collect the photo-copy of Macmillan's brilliant Parliamentary answer in that distant, civilised past. Dealing with young Mr Dalyell's demand for legislation to be drafted in less obscure language, the Prime Minister had replied that since legislation was often the subject of litigation, it was necessary not only that it should appear to be simple to those who read it in good faith, but actually precise. Many things in this life looked simple enough. Take, for example, the following sentence:

'When John met his uncle in the street he took off his hat.'

That was a clear sentence, Macmillan had said, yet it was capable of at least six different meanings. We chortled over this linguistic joke. Yes, how apt; how clever. And when I came to think of it, how like one of Mr Dalyell's own sentences.

A Fear of Poverty

SIR MONTY FINNISTON

Even at the age of 76, Sir Monty Finniston has a full diary. At one point in my dealings with his formidable secretary, the best on offer was an hour with Sir Monty in an airport lounge at the end of another hard day's business. His entry in Who's Who is a staggering record of hyper-activity. Garlanded with honours, he is still chairman or director of more than a dozen organisations, with interests ranging from oil and property to prison reform and nutrition.

"What the hell do I have to look forward to? Actuarially? How many more years? At the end, people will forget me. But I've still got to satisfy myself that I've done something."

"So working at full stretch has always been terribly important to you?"

"Yes. It's a throwback." He gave a little laugh. "I'm scared of being poor. I've got no reason to be, because I live very comfortably. But I am scared. And I don't like to see poverty in others."

Sir Monty's fear of poverty goes back a long way. The Gorbals boy who became Chairman of the British Steel Corporation and Chancellor of Stirling University began life in a squalid top-floor tenement, the oldest of five children of a Russian-born Jew whose real name he never discovered.

"I've heard all kinds of stories. I'm not quite sure. The name is spelt differently from the district of Finnieston. That's spelt with an 'e'. People say, and I think it's true, that my father's name originally was Finestein."

"Was he a great influence on you?"

"None at all. He was a tailor by profession. If that is a profession. But he worked as a commercial traveller, and was very rarely at home. My mother influenced me more."

"Was it a religious upbringing?"

"Religion played a big part in my life. There must have been four or five synagogues in the Gorbals in those days. It was a real Jewish enclave. Of course the Jews became rich and moved south. To Newton Mearns, Eaglesham, places like that. I don't think there are any synagogues in the Gorbals now. The Pakistanis and the Sikhs have taken their place."

"What else do you remember of the Gorbals?"

"The tenements weren't anything to boast about. No bath, no hot water. A toilet on the landing which served three apartments on the top floor. People with motor cars were quite unusual. If you earned £1,000 a year you were a rich man. There was high unemployment, and no welfare state. But the steel works were doing very well, and metallurgists were people who made money."

He was a bright boy. He gained a scholarship to Allan Glen's School, then a first-class honours degree at Glasgow University. He decided he would be a metallurgist.

"I don't think my parents were very happy about that. They thought that you'd never get out unless you were a lawyer or a doctor or a teacher."

Sir Monty, pink and relaxed, sitting eagerly on the edge of a sofa in his suite of offices in an elegant London square, and speaking in that curiously high, keen Glaswegian voice which he reminded me proudly that he had never lost, made his boyhood sound like a term of imprisonment with eventual release something that had to be worked for and willed. Later in the conversation, I asked him about an odd and overlooked aspect of his public work — his campaigning on behalf of prisoners. His answer might have been expected. He said he objected to men having to urinate and defecate inside a cell. He said that took him back to the Gorbals and the single toilet on the landing, to the days when a father's best ambition for his son was that he should somehow "get out".

"Was it a happy childhood?"

"No. We didn't suffer from poverty, but we always knew we were poor."

"What's the difference?"

"You don't suffer from poverty if you're dressed, if you eat, and you have music. Then you don't notice you're poor. But you're poor all right, because you look around...and you see..."

Monty Finniston got out. After graduating, he lectured briefly at the Royal College of Science and Technology in Glasgow, quickly realised that he was only mouthing what he had learned as a student, and headed south at the first opportunity. He began his industrial career as a night-shift foreman in Corby. Thirteen years later, he was the Atomic Energy Authority's chief metallurgist at Harwell.

"That was the happiest part of my life. At Harwell, I did all kinds of things for the first time. That was when I was original, when I was thinking. It was lovely. But there were guys working for me who'd been there 30 years. I thought to myself, what the hell are they doing? I had this theory that to stay more than 10 years in any job was the wrong thing to do. For the first three years you learned, for the next three or four you put something in, after that you lost ambition and originality."

He was slightly over his 10-year limit at Harwell, a little under it at the British Steel Corporation.

"What did you learn about managing people?"

"I was impatient. I mean, I had 29 unions in the BSC. I tried to convert them in less than 10 years. Impossible. That was my big fault — trying to do things too hurriedly. But how long am I going to live for? That was it. You're dead a long time."

"Do you approve of what Mrs Thatcher has done to the unions? Tried to smash them?"

"She hasn't smashed the unions," Sir Monty said indignantly. "She hasn't smashed them at all."

"Do you think she should have done?"

"Well, unions are essential, but not the way they're organised at present. Look at all the industrial unrest she's got. And if a Labour government gets in, I don't know what's going to happen. Will the unions play ball?"

"They're worried about unemployment. What's to be done about that?"

"I take this view. A man can't start work aged 18 and retire at 65, without being educated and re-educated, trained and re-trained, several times in his working life. People have to recognise this.

That's point one. Point two is that I don't think people can expect to work as long as they have in the past. My father worked 48 hours a week, 48 weeks in the year, for I don't know how many years. But my son won't. Who does?"

"Yuppies work awfully hard, apparently."

"Well, perhaps. But for most people, the 40-hour week will go to 35."

"What do you think of the present government?"

"I think people should be able to live comfortably. Not too comfortably. I'm not a great believer in wealth. My major impression of the Prime Minister is that she's done very well for the rich. But she's done damn all for the poor. And there are a helluva lot of poor around."

"Are you a political animal?"

"Apolitical. I believe what Adlai Stevenson said. He said that politicians are people who approach every problem with an open mouth."

"Are there any politicians you like?"

"There are some," he said grudgingly. "Not because they're politicians, but because they've got character. I admire John Smith. Very good man. And Michael Foot. And Ted Heath. When I was knighted, Ted Heath wrote from the West Indies to congratulate me. From the West Indies! He didn't have to do that."

Having got out, Monty Finniston preferred to stay out. He has returned regularly to Scotland to fulfil a variety of professional commitments, as chairman of such bodies as the Scottish Business School, Clyde Cablevision and Anderson Strathclyde. But when he returns, he does so as a commuter. If I had met him in an airport lounge, it would have been Glasgow Airport, as he awaited the last flight of the day back to London. It might have been an appropriate setting.

When I asked him about the Scottish Protestant work ethic — whether it still existed, assuming it ever had — Sir Monty said that had disappeared with the welfare state. He had reservations about the welfare state. It had brought things he didn't like — alcohol abuse, hooliganism, drug abuse. Edinburgh was terrible now.

He'd place all that at the door of the welfare state? Well, he reflected, perhaps materialism had a lot to answer for.

"But about this work ethic. Do you think we should be taking a tip from the Japanese who work all the hours God sends?"

About this, Sir Monty was certain. The Scots would never do that. Never.

"Why not?"

"Well, because I think..." He paused. "Well, because," he said, quite benevolently, "I think the Scots are a lazy set of bastards, to be quite frank!"

"As bad as that?"

"Oh, I don't think the work ethic is very strong. And the Scots are very reliant. A couple of years ago, I went around Scotland for the BBC. They wanted me to tell them what Scotland would be like in the year 2000. Well, it was quite clear-cut. All the sunset industries were disappearing, unemployment was bad but nothing exceptional, and high technology had come in. But there wasn't a single Scottish investor. IBM. Hoescht. Olivetti. NEC. NCR. Reo Stakis! A Cypriot! What the hell's he got to do with it? Nothing to do with Scotland! I spoke to a banker and he said to me, 'Oh, banks never invest. We look to interest on principal, and if we get that, we're quite happy'. An eye-opener!"

"So what happened to the enterprising Scots? The innovators?"

"They left Scotland," he said sadly, "that's what happened. What would have happened to Scotland if we'd all stayed?"

"It would have been a better country."

"Yes. We'd have quarrelled with each other. But it would have been better."

"So why did you all leave?"

"No opportunities," he said, staring at the coffee table. "No opportunities."

"We don't seem to invent things any more."

"Perhaps not. It's quite astonishing how much we did."

"But it's all in the past."

"Yes, and I don't really know why. And yet, we've got I don't know how many universities."

"What impression do you get when you go back to Scotland?"

Sir Monty, who had begun to look quite dejected, cheered up. If we were a lazy set of bastards, lacking in enterprise, slavishly reliant on American and Japanese branch factories, at least it seemed that we were happy in our indolence and dependence.

"The people are more normal than they were. Less hangdog. More alive. Look at Glasgow. Incredible! And you know the man who's never got the credit for it?"

"Who?"

"Michael Kelly!" he laughed. "I've said to him, 'Michael, they should have knighted you at least!' And he just shrugs his shoulders. Then of course he goes to Edinburgh and makes a balls of it!"

Three years ago, Sir Monty Finniston was asked to deliver a lecture on business ethics. With his usual thoroughness and dedication to the task in hand, he decided to read the Bible from cover to cover. What had his research taught him?

"These people knew nothing about pulsars, or quasars, or stars, or the size of the universe, or atoms, or particles. There were no international exchanges 3,000 years ago. They lived in little villages, with no transport at all. And yet in the Bible, you can pick out lots of sentences which tell you what to do. They believed in paying for labour. They believed in trade unions. They believed in not over-charging. Marks and Spencer charges 29 per cent APR. They would have considered that usury. They believed you shouldn't charge more than 16 per cent on the cost of your article, and if you did, you paid the guy back. All this, and a bit more besides. Three thousand years ago! Long before we knew about all these things! So these chaps had a character, a morality, a view of life. But people don't pay any attention to it..."

"You said that as a child, religion played a big part in your life. Are you religious now?"

"I don't know, I don't know. I'm a scientist by profession, and there's no evidence of God. But curiously enough, Hawking, this fellow from Cambridge who's written the book A Brief History of Time...he has a very interesting proposition. He believes in a creator. Not a man with a beard in the sky, of course...but some kind of creation. Otherwise, he says, how can you account for the weight of the neutron or the proton or the electron, or the charges in them? Because if they'd been slightly higher or slightly lower, we wouldn't have had the world. That's a very interesting comment, isn't it?"

"Do you agree with him?"

"Well, I'm agnostic on the point. I mean, I practise my religion, but I'm not wedded to it."

"Apart from the Bible and Stephen Hawking, do you read a lot?"

"Oh, yes. I don't sleep too much. Three hours a night. Which got me into a row. What happened was, I went to this party, and a chap said to me, 'You only sleep three hours a night? Do you know Mrs Thatcher only sleeps five hours a night?' 'No,' I said, 'I didn't know that. I've never slept with Mrs Thatcher!' This guy got bloody angry! And I thought I was being very clever! Then, as well as reading, I think about things. When you're awake, and nobody's with you, you're quite alone, then you can think quite deeply about things..."

"What do you think about science?"

"That it's not enough. Science is not enough. I don't think just doing science is necessarily an answer to everything. Otherwise, we would never have charities, would we? We would never look after the sick or the poor. Because these things are not economically sensible. They can't be justified in that way. But we do justify them. We do look after the sick and the poor."

We were back to the fear of poverty. We had never been far away.

A Pint on the Terrace

CHARLES KENNEDY

"Let's meet for a pint on the terrace," Charles Kennedy suggested when I telephoned for an interview. "Then, if you like, I'll get you a ticket for Scottish Questions in the afternoon."

"That sounds fun."

"Fun," said the young Democrat MP for Ross, Cromarty and Skye, "is not exactly the word I'd choose to describe Scottish Questions."

By 1 p.m. on the appointed day, Mr Kennedy was one of the few MPs above ground. There had been an all-night sitting. Having got to bed at 6 a.m., he was back on the premises four hours later to greet a party of constituents from the Royal British Legion, Drumnadrochit. Such are the joys of political life.

In the circumstances, he was looking remarkably chipper. Tall and red-haired, he has something of the Highland warrior about him. But he talks like a lowlander.

He took me to the Strangers Bar, where I immediately committed a social gaffe by offering to buy the long-awaited pint. "The first thing I'll do when I'm Prime Minister," he said, pointing to a notice, "is to get this silly rule changed." The notice forbids strangers to buy or order drink, and advises members not to leave strangers unaccompanied for more than 15 minutes at a time. When Mr Kennedy disappeared to fetch sandwiches, I wondered idly what might happen to me if my host was unexpectedly delayed in some distant canteen.

"How many bars are there in this building?"

"Nineteen," he said. "But I've only managed to track down 12."

A number of pin-striped gentlemen at the bar — for some reason I took them to be Conservatives — were laughing heartily. We agreed that, even on this chilly June afternoon, the terrace might be a better bet. Sure enough, it was deserted. We sat at a table as far as possible from the river's edge, nibbled brown salad sandwiches, and drank our pints. Charles Kennedy asked if I minded him smoking.

"You must be depressed by the state of the polls in Scotland," I suggested. "According to yesterday's Glasgow Herald, support for the SSLD has slipped to 5%."

"SS for short!" he replied jovially, lighting up.

What was this? A politician cracking jokes at the expense of his own side? I was already beginning to understand why a political commentator once described Mr Kennedy as one of the few fully paid-up members of the human race in the Palace of Westminster.

"People are still confused about who's what," he said. "Curiously enough, the collapse of David Owen's party base has probably had a knock-on effect on us. People think we're folding our tents as well."

"It doesn't help that the name is so difficult to remember."

"We should have called ourselves the Alliance. We'd spent the best part of five years marketing that. But during the merger talks, we couldn't get that, and ended up with this lowest common denominator title, the Social and Liberal Democrats. It'll just take time. We've got to keep plugging away and not get too depressed."

Mr Kennedy was the first SDP MP to join the merged centre party after the 1987 general election. I said I remembered being slightly surprised at the speed with which he had distanced himself from David Owen when faced with the choice. Had he had any doubts?

"Not really. Immediately after the election, David Steel moved too fast with his merger proposals, but then David Owen bounced back with an equally counter-productive reaction. Really, it was merger or bust. If we hadn't merged, it would have been a complete shambles. You may say it's been a complete shambles anyway, but I think it would have been even worse."

"Was it a bad time for you personally?"

"It was. Not that David Owen ever made it personally unpleasant for me. But at that stage, I was the only one of the five to go. It was extremely dejecting and draining."

"Do you and David Owen still speak amicably?"

"Amicably enough, but I couldn't say that we've had a conversation of any serious substance for a couple of years. It's been a fairly fundamental rift."

"Personally, as well as politically?"

Mr Kennedy had a think about that. "Well..." There was a further pause. "Yes," he said finally.

"Do you still admire him?"

"Very much so. What should have happened is that we should have merged, and he should have been the leader."

"Do you think he would have been elected?"

"I do."

"Even if David Steel had stood against him?"

"There was a general recognition that of the two, David Owen was the man with the greater capacity for the leadership. I think he would have won. Had that happened, there would have been no split, no separate party, we might well have overtaken Labour in the polls last year, and the whole landscape would have looked quite different. Anyhow, the benefit of hindsight is a wonderful thing."

"Perhaps, though, David Owen didn't think he would be elected leader. Might that have been a factor?"

"He told me privately at the time that he did think he would have become leader but that he simply wasn't convinced by merger."

"So it was purely a stand on principle?"

"It seems to have been. The whole thing has been a tragic mistake from his point of view. I still think he's the most talented figure in opposition politics. He's head and shoulders above Kinnock, no doubt about that. I mean, you'll hear that from a number of Labour MPs sotto voce. But I'm afraid his talents are just being wasted now."

"You share the view he's committed political suicide?"

"I think he personally can survive, but I don't see how he can get himself into a position where he'll be part of a viable political group again. Unless, of course, he rejoins the Labour Party."

I felt that it was time to talk about something more cheerful.

★ ★ ★

It is said that in the Highlands they elect personalities, not parties. On that basis, Charles Kennedy has a seat for life. His family has been crofting in Lochaber for centuries. His grandfather campaigned in the Gaelic-speaking counties for Johnny Bannerman, one of the great men of Scottish Liberalism. His father still runs the family croft, although, like most crofters, he also has a full-time job (with the North of Scotland Hydro-Electric Board). Charles is the youngest of three children.

"There's a bit of a gap between me and my older brother and sister — about eight years — so I was always used to being brought up with older people around. My sister's quite political, perhaps slightly left of me, and my first interest came from just listening to discussion at home. But I'm probably the first member of the family to be a member of a political party."

At the age of 29, Mr Kennedy has already been a member of three political parties. He joined the Labour Party when he was 15 and one of Lochaber High School's star debaters.

"If the revolution ever does come, I don't think it'll start in Fort William." He puffed thoughtfully at his cigarette. "Come to that, I don't think it'll even reach Fort William."

"When did you drop out of Labour?"

"After a couple of years at university. The Labour club at Glasgow didn't participate in student debating. Too bourgeois and middle-class for them. At that point, the Labour Party nationally was going to hell after 1979. I just couldn't believe it. Here was this rapacious right-wing Tory government. You'd have thought that Labour would just have sat back and waited to win the next election."

Unimpressed by the Labour boycott, he went on to win the Observer Mace for university debating, as John Smith and Donald Dewar had done before him. But he was never tempted to follow these distinguished predecessors into the law. He really wanted to be a journalist. Instead, he almost ended up a banker.

"I was offered the post of Grade 2 management trainee with Lloyds Bank," he said, "although I'm the last person who should ever have gone into banking. Then I got a Fulbright scholarship to Indiana, and they said they'd hold the job for a year." By the time Lloyds Bank contacted him again, their Grade 2 management trainee had become Britain's youngest MP. "I couldn't resist writing to them from the House of Commons saying I was otherwise engaged. They never replied. No sense of humour!"

"You would have been a bad banker. Would you have been a good journalist?"

"OK, probably."

"You could have ended up reporting Parliament, perhaps?"

Mr Kennedy's face brightened suddenly.

"There's actually still a large part of me that enjoys the observation of politics as much as the engagement in it."

"Is that a good thing?"

"Well, I don't think you can take the poacher-gamekeeper act too far. But yes. When John Biffen was described as a semi-detached member of the government, I thought that was a great compliment."

We both laughed at the irony, as he continued: "Although it appears to have been the final nail in his coffin!"

"What you're saying is that it's possible to take politics too seriously?"

"The happiest politicians are the ones, not necessarily with other jobs, but with other pursuits. It just gives you a degree of balance. Like having a chip on both shoulders."

"Someone did say that politicians had to have something in their lives that was more important than politics."

"That's absolutely right."

"So what is it in your case?" (Mr Kennedy is unmarried.)

"I do like writing, doing the odd column, or the occasional bit of freelance broadcasting. That's great. Apart from that, I have a very romantic notion, which may never be fulfilled, to get the family croft at Fort William back into full production. When my grandfather was alive, there were cows. Now only potatoes."

Two gentlemen in clean macs ambled towards us. One produced a card and announced himself as the new political editor of Mr Rupert Murdoch's Today newspaper. His companion was from the Scotsman. They looked like minor characters out of an obscure French film.

Mr Kennedy politely accepted the card, and the pair slouched off. Our conversation resumed without any reference to these unexpected visitors.

* * *

The Ross, Cromarty and Skye result was the last to be declared in the 1983 general election. Around lunchtime on the Friday, I was in a BBC studio in Glasgow, presenting a hangover round-up of late results, when an excited reporter dashed into the studio and announced that there had been a major upset in the Highlands.

"Charlie who?" I asked. Charlie Who was 23.

"Did you expect to win the seat?"

"No. I thought we'd come a magnificent second."

"What do you remember of your first day here?"

"The first duty of the new House was to elect a Speaker. The place was packed. I had a feeling of complete unreality. In walked Michael Foot, Ted Heath, Jim Callaghan. That was when it hit me. Up till then, I had been slightly nonplussed. Then I realised that I was part of this as well. It did take a lot of getting used to."

"It's easy to become overwhelmed?"

"It can be. And I was also concerned about being the youngest member. I thought that could be a poisoned chalice. So I spent a lot of time asking advice. Quite simple, mechanical things. And what I discovered was that as long as you're willing to ask them, they're willing to give you the time. That goes for all parties."

"Who are the politicians of other parties that you like?"

"There's Tam (Dalyell), certainly. He's a great force for good in this place. Fantastic back-bench MP. The abilities of John Smith and Gordon Brown are not in question. And the other Labour MP I have a great deal of time for is Frank Field. Absolutely outstanding in his analysis and understanding, particularly of social policy. On the government side, Malcolm Rifkind is an able politician, there's no doubt about that. I used to admire Kenneth Clarke more than I do now. He's just becoming too heavy-handed. The thing that strikes me about the Tory Party is this great temptation among ministers to play along with the Thatcherite breeze. So you see quite sensible people behaving in a silly, obnoxious way."

"Did you find that you liked the House of Commons?"

"It wasn't unwelcoming, it wasn't unpleasant. But I thought it would be the bee's knees, you know? The ultimate. But it wasn't at all. It surprised me that I wasn't nearly as fond of the chamber as I thought I'd be."

"Why not?"

"I think partly because as a member of a third party, you don't have the mass battalions behind you. But also because the more I saw the place, the more I realised I fundamentally disagreed with much of what goes on here, the way things are done. Procedure, lack of accountability, lack of scrutiny, lack of democracy in the place itself. Scottish Question Time today. As a Scottish MP, you get the chance of one oral question to a Scottish Office minister once a month, if you're lucky. There's no way in the world that's doing your job properly."

"And the hours?" Mr Kennedy, after his sleepless night and early morning visitation from the Royal British Legion, Drumnadrochit, was beginning to wilt.

"Yes, we were here till half past five this morning, voting on something that nobody outside is going to thank you for. One of the things I don't like about establishment politics, be it of the left or of the right, is that they all want to change things. But the one thing they don't want to change is the way they do things. Everybody else has to change but them. I've never found that a persuasive slogan."

The more we talked, the more Biffen-like in his detachment did he sound. The word I was going to use was disillusioned. Not quite yet, perhaps. But when he went on to recall how Roy Jenkins's vision of political realignment — something about an aeroplane about to take off — had first attracted him into the SDP, it was difficult to believe that those stirring mould-breaking days had ever really happened. They seem now as baffling and transitory as the men with the business cards. Now you see them, now you don't. If Mr Kennedy is a disappointed politician, he is entitled to be. He has been let down by older heads, but not necessarily wiser ones.

"What's the political philosophy of the new party? Does it have one?"

"Yes, it does."

"People don't know what it is."

"Quite agree, but we've got to be careful not to confuse people by saying that our political philosophy is different from what it was at the time of the Alliance. I don't think it is, really. It's the same people, minus a few, standing for much the same kind of policies. An effective, competitive economy, more social justice, strong commitment to internationalism, and underpinning the whole thing, complete constitutional overhaul. That is where we are on the spectrum."

"Is there a lot separating that tick-list from Neil Kinnock's Labour Party?"

"I think there is basically, because if you look at Labour's policy review, the public face — the smile on the face of the tiger — will be committed to all sorts of things that nobody could disagree with. I don't believe the Labour Party as an institution believes in half of it. In government, as soon as the going got difficult, anything up to a quarter of his Parliamentary party would be in complete rebellion. Fifty Labour MPs have already signed an open letter saying they won't accept anything less than unilateralism."

"Do you have ambitions to lead your party?"

"No, I can't honestly say it appeals to me."

"But you wouldn't object if you were prevailed upon?"

"I'm not sure I would be prevailed upon. In 10, 20 years' time, I might think differently. But I've seen David Steel, Robert Maclennan and David Owen at close quarters trying to do this third party leadership job. It's a killer. It's got all the hassle of Secretary of State for Northern Ireland with none of the rewards."

It was 2.15: almost time for the monthly opportunity to ask Mr Rifkind a question. We retreated indoors to the Strangers Bar, and gossiped. He told me that he enjoyed gossip, particularly with friends over a meal; he found that as relaxing as anything else.

Walking with me to the lift which transports members of the public to the Strangers Gallery, he asked me whether I had ever thought about entering politics.

"You should think about it," he said. "When we get a Scottish parliament."

"What makes you think we will?"

"Oh, I think it'll happen," he said.

Such is his wholly engaging scepticism that by the time we had reached the lift, he was no longer as confident in his prediction. But if we did get a parliament in Edinburgh, 49-year-old Charles Kennedy would, I feel sure, make a wonderful Prime Minister.

Out of the Filing Cabinet

TOM CONTI

"The first time I saw you on stage was many years ago at the Edinburgh Festival. It was in a play by Cecil Taylor, but I can't remember what it was called..."

"It was called the Black and White Minstrels," said Tom Conti. "One of the best plays I've ever done."

A sly send-up of middle-class liberal values, it was not only extremely funny but outrageously vulgar. It might have contained more expletives than any other play in the English language.

"The stage manager counted them one night. He made it 296. Give or take 10 a night, because it changed from performance to performance. One improvised to some extent." He recited with some relish one outstandingly indecent line.

"You liked Cecil Taylor as a playwright?"

"And as a man. His death was a tragic loss. He had such a fine gift for metaphor — encapsulating a whole social structure into a domestic situation. That needs a lot of skill and imagination. He had all of that."

It is hard to accept that our mutual friend is dead. When I think of him, I still picture him sweating out scripts in a hut at the bottom of his garden in the wilds of Northumberland. He was a craftsman at doing one of the most difficult things in the world — earning a living as a full-time playwright.

Although he was a Scot, Cecil Taylor preferred not to live in Scotland. He once told me he breathed a sigh of relief when the train from Glasgow crossed the border. I wondered if Tom Conti felt the same.

"Not really. I couldn't live in Scotland because I would starve to death if I did. I make my living all over the shop, and this (London) seems to be the place where you have to centralise — which is the great curse of all Scottish actors. They all have to make this horrendous decision. And of course the old problem of accent always crops up. If you want to work in other than Scottish theatre, you have to be able to lose your accent. The only way to do that effectively is to leave Scotland, and be able to switch it on or off."

In fact, Tom Conti is one of the few Scottish actors I know whose consonants do not sound artificially Anglicised. His natural speech is still unaffectedly Scottish, which is not the least of his attractive qualities.

But I didn't want us to get side-tracked into a debate on accents. I was still thinking about Cecil Taylor.

"Maybe the reason Cecil lived in England was because he found Scotland such a suffocating place."

"I would agree with that."

"Why is it suffocating?"

"I don't know what the root of the problem is. Maybe it's England. I'm no Anglophobe, but any interference in another country's development is catastrophic. It increases insularity. It increases anger. But there is a parallel question. Why is religion so uppermost in Scottish consciousness?"

Now perhaps we were getting warm. Like Cecil Taylor, he was brought up as a member of a racial/religious minority in the west of Scotland. Taylor was a Glaswegian Jew; Tom Conti is half-Italian and received a Catholic education. But before we could explore these interesting connections, and consider their possible relationship to the suffocating atmosphere of Scottish life, we were interrupted by a tree surgeon in deepest Hampstead.

"I'd better see that man before he goes," Mr Conti said anxiously, leaping from his chair. We were sitting in the studio of his London home, overlooking a large, pretty, wooded garden. "He's been having a look at an oak tree."

While he was away, I drank coffee from a Radio 4 mug and surveyed the scene: a grand piano upon which someone had been playing Mozart's Sonata in G; a half-finished canvas resting on an easel; a wire hanging from the ceiling without a bulb at the end of it; a word processor in the corner; a dilapidated armchair with a guitar on it; wall shelves packed with discs; and a sofa with a plump cushion at one end and no cushion at the other. From the cushioned end, I observed the householder and the tree surgeon in earnest conversation in the garden.

He returned full of apologies for having kept me waiting.

"What's the verdict, then?"

"It'll have to go," he replied sadly. "It's 300 years old and they're going to have to take it down. It's in danger of crashing into the neighbour's house."

His melancholy eyes were more melancholy than ever.

"Tell me about your parents. Your father was Italian, your mother Scottish?"

"Yes. They were emotionally very uncluttered people, which is responsible in large part for my own contentment. I'm not a neurotic; nor were they. But there's no doubt that what my father went through with internment during the war shortened his life."

"Internment?"

"The night Italy came into the war, he was taken away. There was no time to say goodbye to my mother. Just boots on the stair and a knock on the door."

"How did your mother react?"

"They had a ladies' hairdressers in Paisley and lived above the shop. They used to make shampoo for use in the shop — boiled the stuff in zinc pails. So she went down to the shop in a panic, put boiling water in these zinc pails, and left the pails on the window sill along the front of the building. She was going to repel anybody who came to make trouble. She was going to protect the castle. Pretty feisty woman!"

"And did anybody come to make trouble?"

"The following morning, she opened the shop as usual. By then she was like a zombie. Word had got out pretty fast, and people came to ask if there was anything they could do to help. So there was never any trouble. Only support."

"Where was your father sent?"

"To the Isle of Man. Churchill tried to get rid of the problem of these unruly people, these thugs and vagabonds, and asked the Canadian government to take them off his hands. They were ice cream merchants, hairdressers, shopkeepers, people like that — anything less thug-like could not be imagined. But they were put on a ship for Canada, the ship was torpedoed in the Atlantic, and most of them drowned. My father wasn't on the boat, but all his friends with one exception died."

"Your father was kept on the Isle of Man?"

"Yes, he was diabetic and not well. My mother thought, probably rightly, that he would die. There was no special diet — nothing. So she went with my grandfather to see a high-ranking police officer. She took with her a suitcase containing £2,000. And she said to this police officer, 'You can have this, if you get my husband out of the Isle of Man.'"

"Did he?"

"He did," said Tom Conti in a low voice. "Terrifying."

"What do you make of the story?"

"It took amazing courage to go with that suitcase. And although it was a phenomenally serious crime, they didn't have any moral problem about it at all. He wasn't an alien anyway. For God's sake, he'd lived in this country for 21 years. If he'd been able-bodied, he'd probably have joined up. But they remained in terror until the day they died."

"In case it came out?"

"Yes. One day years later — it was a Sunday and my father was in the garden — the police came to the door. 'Is Alfonso Conti there?' My mother said later she didn't know how she got down to the garden. They thought that was it — that they were both going to be taken to jail for a thousand years and that I would be orphaned. 'Sorry to tell you,' said the policeman, 'but there's been a break-in at your shop.' Best news my father ever had!"

"Did he ever talk to you about his experience?"

"A little bit. About doors being opened, food being thrown on the ground. It was a nightmare for him."

The Contis sent their only child to a small private school in Glasgow called Hamilton Park.

"It might have worked quite well," he said, "if it hadn't been shackled to religion."

"There was a lot of religion, was there?"

"God, yes. Never-ending. A lot of religion but very little Christianity."

"Yes, that's an important distinction."

"It sure is."

"Was it a tough education?"

"Well, the Lochgelly (tawse) was very much in evidence. Pointless way to deal with children. But it wasn't harsh. Not like a public school. There wasn't a terrific amount of bullying or anything. And a lot of the teachers were really quite nice."

"Did you believe in God?"

"Yes," he replied immediately — then swithered. "Well, I don't know if I believed. But I was told in no uncertain terms He was there. It was the old Jesuit thing. Give me a child..."

"Was this your teachers, or your parents, or both?"

"My parents weren't religious. That was the balance which saved me, really. My father didn't ever go to church, he just didn't like it. He'd seen Italy, and priests, and all the rest of it. He was no great lover of the clergy, he thought the whole thing was dishonest. I agree with him."

"That priests are dishonest?"

"Not that all priests are dishonest, no. But the base of it is, I think."

"How?"

"Well, it's a tremendous ruse really, isn't it? 'If you give me what you have, I will promise you eternal happiness — later!'" Mr Conti chuckled to think about it. "And somehow they fall for it. I can't believe that they continue to fall for it, but they do — there's no logic to any of it."

"When people suffered, it was something to look forward to. Eternity, I mean."

"That's right. The church helped them to suffer. The church and state went hand in hand for so long. It was all part of running the same business."

"What about the separateness of Catholic education?"

"Feel strongly about that. It's absolutely appalling! Any separateness is just bad. It's...it's a waterfall of acid over everything. It doesn't allow people to develop their thinking ability."

"What effect has it had on Scottish society? An unhealthy effect, you would say?"

"Extraordinarily so." But he was keen to search for deeper explanations of our religious prejudices than segregated education alone. "What is it that makes Scotland like that? It is so immediately evident. Go to Scotland and you start hearing words like 'Catholic' and 'Protestant'. You never hear those words down here. You never hear them! But as soon as you're over the border — you're a Catholic!"

"Do you think the Scots have a special respect for education?"

"People in the south still believe we do, although it's probably a bit of a myth. But the one terrific thing about Scottish education is that fathers are as enthusiastic about the education of their daughters as of their sons. That separates Scotland from almost every other country in the world."

"Were you happy as a child?"

"Very happy. Partly because of my parents, partly because of the children I knew. An amazingly happy bunch."

"Have you remained happy?"

"Yes. A good marriage."

"You're not a typical actor, then?"

"No. But it might have turned out differently if Kara (his wife) hadn't been around. We think exactly the same way."

"You say your parents weren't religious. Were they political?"

"Not really. But they did talk about — this word — 'the government'. I never quite understood as a child what 'the government' was. But whatever it was, it was bad. Even when it changed, it was bad. My father always said he thought people were generally better off under Labour. He could tell that by the number of times the shop door opened. But traditionally they voted Tory. At least, my father said he voted Tory. I suspect he actually voted Labour!"

"Are you interested in politics?"

"Not in the machinery of politics, but I am interested in how people are and why they are. This education thing — the destruction of the thinking ability — is very important. Educating the populace is really anathema to all parties everywhere. Nobody wants to educate the populace. Not really educate them. Sure, in the Soviet Union they're all crackingly good at multiplication. But there's a whole section of the brain that's been lopped off. Same here. Sometimes I wonder if I should actually do something about it."

"Like what?"

"Maybe think of changing careers and go into politics. But I hate party politics so much that I can't think what party I would join. It certainly wouldn't be the Tories."

Sitting there in his faded jeans, his old jumper and his open-necked blue shirt, Tom Conti did not look to me like one of Mr Kinnock's besuited army of the Nineties. But I have a fancy that in the fullness of time he might be a splendid ally of Charles Kennedy. Kennedy and Conti: what a charismatic ticket that would make.

"How did you get interested in the theatre? Was it a theatre-going family?"

"Oh, yes. Though I remember theatre-going more in London than in Glasgow. My parents went to London a couple of times a year to keep up with all the latest fashions in crazy things like permanent waving. I went with them, and every night for a week we'd go to the theatre. We saw everything from Agatha Christie to T.S. Eliot."

"Who were your favourites?"

"One night we saw a play called The Confidential Clerk, and in it was an actor called Denholm Elliott. As soon as I saw this man I thought, 'He's different from everybody else.' I wondered why. Then I realised that what was different about him was that he was the best actor I'd ever seen. I'd seen lots of actors who were very good, jolly and charming on the stage, terrific performers. But this guy wasn't just a performer. He was an actor. Curious animal."

"What makes this curious animal?"

Tom Conti gave one of his high, infectious laughs. "That's terribly difficult," he said. "It's got to do with showing you something about the character that you don't normally see. Something that a personality performer wouldn't show you."

"What?"

"Something to do with danger. I think it's an ability to slightly frighten the audience. Olivier had it. Certainly Denholm has it. All really fine actors have it. A feeling of unease — that excites an audience."

"Who else do you like among your peers?"

"Michael Gambon is terrific. Walter Matthau. De Niro.

Hoffman. There are so many."

"So it was going to the theatre with your parents that gave you a desire to be part of it?"

"That, and the fact that performing got me out of tricky situations as a child. I was terribly small until I was 14, and when you're little you tend to be set upon sometimes. But if you could tell a joke, you survived."

"Are there any distinctive characteristics about Scottish acting?"

"When I was there, Scots actors had a very no-nonsense approach to their work. Not so arty as down here. We thought of it more as a practical craft — and if there was a bit of artistry to it as well, then jolly good. I was lucky enough to work with people like Walter Carr, John Grieve, Leonard Maguire and Roddy Macmillan. All terrific craftsmen. When they were getting a laugh, they knew how to get it. There was nothing accidental about it."

A few years ago, Tom Conti returned to the west of Scotland to make a film (Heavenly Pursuits) with Helen Mirren. The experience was a shock to the system.

"When I left Glasgow, it was a dark and dying city, absolutely hopeless. You could feel it. The yards were closing, nothing was happening, buildings were being razed. It was as if somebody had gone out and cut down all the trees in the garden out of sheer rage. Going back was astonishing. There was a whole different feel to Glasgow — a feeling of life and determination. But outside the city, what I saw really shook me. I walked through Paisley one day and saw a downtrodden people. Mouths turned down, eyes dead...totally haggard."

"And that's not how you remembered them?"

"No, but I wasn't observant in my childhood."

"So maybe they were downtrodden then, too."

"Maybe. But the awful thing is that they still are. Of course it's not just Paisley. I'm sure if you went to Birmingham, you'd find some doon in the mooth craturs walking about there as well."

"Why?"

Mr Conti in his reply became quite impassioned. "Because people feel they have no control over their own lives, that they're boxed in. Filing cabinet living. Whether they're working in one or living in one, someone's put them in a bloody filing cabinet. They do hopeless, repetitive jobs — and they're not allowed to have their say. But in the end it always come back to the same basic thing."

"What?"

"Education. If people are encouraged to think — not what to think, just to think — then they'll be able to think their way out of their terrible situations. And as the need for labour becomes less and less, the need for a thinking population becomes more and more."

It had been a bad week for Tom Conti. The oak tree was about to be felled, and he had just suffered a serious setback in his professional life. A film project dear to his heart — a screen version of Noel Coward's comedy Present Laughter, which he was to have directed and starred in — had been abandoned after a year's preparatory work. Though he was flying to New York the following day to see if anything could be salvaged, he was not hopeful.

As he drove me in his open-topped sports car to Hampstead tube station, I muttered something banal about not having his troubles to seek. That was true, he said — the cancellation of the film had been a personal disaster. On the other hand, his daughter (and only child) had just passed her exams with flying colours; he and Kara were particularly delighted about that.

If Mr Conti does pursue a political career, I see him as a reforming Secretary of State for Education.

A Present for Mrs Thatcher

VERY REV. JAMES WHYTE

"We didn't know what she was going to say, but we did know there would be strong objections to her being allowed to speak at all." At a year's remove, Professor James Whyte reflected calmly on his first few minutes as Moderator of the General Assembly of the Church of Scotland. Upstairs in the place reserved for very important persons was none other than the Prime Minister, awaiting her call to address the ministers and elders at their annual meeting in Edinburgh. "We could have failed to notice her. In that case she would have sat up there with her speech and never delivered it."

He permitted himself a wry smile as he contemplated the possibility of the national church having the temerity not to notice Mrs Margaret Thatcher. Professor Whyte, as well as being one of the most distinguished men in the Church of Scotland, is also one of the nicest. He decided there was no reason to be discourteous to a Prime Minister, and diplomatically avoided a vote on the matter.

"So she came and delivered this long, carefully worked out speech which none of us had really been expecting — bringing a theological justification of her political position into the Assembly. I had to thank her for it, and presented her with a couple of reports which had recently been published by the Church."

"What were they?"

"One on the distribution of wealth and welfare benefits, the other on housing Scotland's people."

"You were trying to tell the Prime Minister something?"

"We were trying to show her that we didn't necessarily agree with everything she said."

The gospel according to Mrs Thatcher was an overnight sensation. The speech was televised live, reprinted in newspapers, endlessly discussed and dissected in and out of Westminster. A year and a half later, her Sermon on the Mound has become one of the standard points of reference to the Thatcher era. But in the Church itself, reaction was subdued. Professor Whyte's moderatorial year was quickly overtaken by a personal tragedy; other leading churchmen stayed silent for their own reasons. The moment passed.

"It's a great pity," James Whyte agreed. "It did require a considered answer, but it still hasn't been given one."

"So tell me. Is her reading of scripture reliable?"

"Oh, no. It's the most extraordinary reading of scripture. The quotation she used, 'If a man will not work, he shall not eat', comes out of a totally different context from ours."

"You mean that society was different?"

"St Paul was dealing with a situation where people lay around and did nothing because they thought the end of the world was coming. Paul said, 'Look, you can't go on living like that. If you're not going to work, you're going to starve.' A totally different situation."

We sat at a table by the window in the living room of Professor Whyte's house in Hope Street, St Andrews, a long, grey, dignified terrace a few minutes' walk from the Old Course. He retired in 1987 as Professor of Practical Theology and Christian Ethics at St Andrews University. When we met, he had just completed his year as Moderator. Time, at last, to reflect.

"Is there any theological objection to Mrs Thatcher's view that we must use our talents to create wealth?"

Professor Whyte, a gentle, bespectacled figure in an open-necked shirt, replied in a soft voice sometimes scarcely louder than a whisper. He thought there was very little in the Bible to justify such an attitude. The New Testament was about poverty rather than wealth, about giving things away and the dangers of wealth. He offered a quotation which had been missing from Mrs Thatcher's scriptural repertoire: 'How shall they that are rich enter the Kingdom of Heaven?'

"What does the Old Testament have to say on the subject?"

"There is a great deal in the Old Testament about prosperity being a blessing of God and God's blessing coming to those who order their life right. But then the Old Testament is all about society, and according to the present Prime Minister, society doesn't exist. The truth is, she confuses the creation of wealth with the making of money."

"How do you define the difference?"

"Wealth," he said slowly, looking down at the beautiful table, "is created by those who take something of no value and make it into something of great value. It's created by craftsmen, by people who work in industry. The shuffling around of shares in order to make yourself a fortune in a fortnight is not wealth creation, it's just making money. She doesn't seem to know the difference."

I had begun this part of our conversation by asking Professor Whyte whether politics interested him very much. He replied yes, in the sense that politics was about how society was ordered, how people were treated, the way laws impinged upon our lives — these were important religious questions; but no, if I meant party politics. "The health of democracy depends on the floating voter," he said. "I've endeavoured to be one." But the more the conversation unfolded, the less likely it seemed that Professor Whyte would be floating in the direction of the Thatcher government.

"Was there anything about the speech you liked?"

"The things she said about the family were fair enough. We all believe in the family!" He gave one of his rare laughs, before adding: "I'm very grateful for my own family."

"Anything else?"

"Some of the things she said about education I would agree with, though that doesn't mean I agree with all government policies on education. The stress on vocational education seems to me to be ludicrous and destructive. It's like the man who sent a postcard to William Temple, the great Archbishop of Canterbury, when Temple worked for the WEA. The man wrote, 'Don't teach my boy poetry. He's going to be a grocer.' The idea that workers don't need poetry is terrible."

"What do you think about the fiercely competitive spirit that the government seems to be encouraging?"

"I'm not against all competitiveness. Such is human sin, human beings need some kind of stimulus to make them work, make them responsible. But I agree with you, this is becoming a fiercely competitive society, and the real problem is the ruthlessness of society towards its failures. What we had with the welfare state, with all its faults and inefficiencies, was a society which showed a care and concern for the weak and the poor. We've lost that. We've lost it already. There are people sleeping in cardboard cities. People who are terribly afraid because the level of benefits is so reduced. There is real poverty now in our country. And if — if — the Health Service is destroyed, we'll end up with an American-style health service where the rich get treatment they don't need and the poor don't get treatment they do need."

He paused, blinked, and lifted his eyes from the table, as if emerging from a meditation.

"I'm becoming very political, aren't I?" he said.

James Whyte speaks with some authority on the subject of society's failures. He was born in Leith 69 years ago, the son of a wholesale provision merchant whose business collapsed in the depression of the 1930s and who, for the rest of his working life, suffered the indignities of the commercial traveller.

When I first asked Professor Whyte about his father, I thought that he might never answer.

"That is a difficult question," he said at last. "My father was a very generous man. He was a man with a sense of failure about him, but also great dignity. A strange mixture." It seemed to me that these few spare words suppressed much emotion.

"And your mother?"

"Her influence was very great," he said, and the atmosphere lifted. "My conversation still is interspersed with her sayings, usually in broad Scots. Also, the fact that we were both left-handed was a bond between us. She always maintained that left-handed people were infinitely superior to any other brand of the human race!"

Although he grew up in a home which was far from wealthy, his parents had a firm sense of duty to their children. He and his two brothers were sent to a fee-paying school — Daniel Stewart's.

"Did you like school?"

"Yes. I was a conformist child. I didn't in those days have much of a streak of rebellion in me. I discovered that if you wanted the approval of your teachers you were good at lessons, but if you wanted the approval of your fellow pupils you played games. I played games. Badly."

"There's a streak of rebellion in you now?"

"I think so, yes. I think I'm much more critical of things than I was then."

"Critical of what?"

"Oh, the conventional things of life. Conventional religion included."

The family was not especially religious, but his parents, lapsed members of the Church of Scotland, did the conventional thing and sent young James to Sunday School. Later he joined an organisation called the Schoolboys' Club, which taught liberal Christianity — what he now describes as "pink politics religion" — at summer camp.

"Suddenly...I remember it yet...we were having a discussion one morning about something in St Matthew's Gospel...and I realised this meant me, that a kind of commitment was required. Essentially in the first instance to the person of Jesus. He sort of got under my skin at that point, and has never got out of it. That was the start of a religious quest for me."

"What did you find?"

Professor Whyte answered the question by telling a small joke against himself. As a young man he had thought he knew everything, and that the world was just waiting to hear what James Whyte would preach. In fact, the first time he stepped into a pulpit, the only comment he got afterwards was, 'They heard you all right at the front, but they didn't hear you very well at the back.'

"You discovered how little you knew?"

"Or how much I didn't know."

He began to see his quest as a process of deepening experience and honesty, compelling him to question his own beliefs.

"The view, for example, that God always rewards the good and punishes the evil. You have to question that, because it's not the way it looks. You have to ask how suffering can be related to God. They told Job, 'You've suffered, so you must have done something wrong.' But you have to think about suffering more deeply than that."

He chose at that moment to think of Lockerbie, where he

preached movingly at the memorial service for the many victims of the Christmas 1988 air disaster.

"This question of evil," I said. "If God is omnipotent, didn't he create the evil?"

"It's the omnipotence of God's love we're dealing with. One can't blame evil on God. Evil relates to the freedom that is given to human beings. Lockerbie was just an act of human wickedness."

Earthquakes, however, he found hard to account for.

At the beginning of the second world war, James Whyte was a pacifist. While a student at Edinburgh University, he moved gradually to an acceptance of the "just war" theory, and came to realise that pacifism for him was no longer tenable: another cherished belief had fallen victim to the quest. He volunteered as a forces chaplain in 1945.

"Do you still believe in the 'just war' theory?"

"I do. I am not even a nuclear pacifist. The nuclear dilemma is a terrible dilemma, but I do believe it has given us a kind of frame within which to make peace."

"Have you ever had any serious crisis of faith?"

"I have doubts all the time about this and that. I discovered one day, for example, that I no longer believed in the virgin birth. It didn't upset me very much. And every time I read about a disaster, I am angry about it. Angry with God. I think that's a natural reaction to evil and disaster, but in the end a belief in God whose love is stronger than evil and whose life is stronger than death — that remains."

"Does it bother you that a lot of good people get by without any religious faith?"

Professor Whyte said he was actually grateful for such people. One of the joys of living and working in a university town for 30 years had been meeting admirable people of various religious faiths and none. Of course, he believed that one day, when they crossed the bourn of death, his atheist friends would open their eyes and say: 'My goodness, yes! It really is!'

"They won't be excluded from the Kingdom?"

"I don't think so, no." And his eyes lit with amusement.

Kind to atheists, he is noticeably less indulgent to some members and fellow ministers of his own flock. Moderators of the General Assembly who are invited at the end of their term of office to give an opinion on the state of the Church usually utter a few anodyne pleasantries. When I asked Professor Whyte the same question, he gave me a reply of startling candour.

"We're almost in danger of becoming a middle-class church. But there's a deeper level of concern. The radical left make people feel guilty because they're not hungry or poor. Well, they do feel guilty, but to make them feel more guilty isn't helping them. The Church should be in the business of releasing people from guilt. From the theological right, on the other hand, it's a kind of personal morality you hear being preached, a very tight package of attitudes and doctrines, a new kind of fundamentalism which is really a very selective way of interpreting the Bible. Ministers who preach these views are not producing the kind of healthy religion that I would like to see."

"Which is?"

"To hear the Gospel really preached, the Gospel of divine grace in Jesus Christ. Then people are released for living. Responsible, healthy living. So much depends on the quality of the preaching."

Two months after he became Moderator, Professor Whyte's wife, Elisabeth, died of cancer.

He cancelled a number of engagements, but decided to go ahead with two services in August, at Helensburgh (commemorating the centenary of the birth of John Logie Baird) and Paisley Abbey. He set himself the test of staying alone in the flat in Edinburgh provided for the Moderator of the General Assembly.

"I was afraid I wouldn't be able to concentrate, wouldn't even be able to sit. To my surprise, I wrote a sermon. But I found I had so much to do I was in danger of not being in touch with my own feelings. Charlotte Square was nice and empty at nights, and when everybody else was away, I could pace around the place and just howl. But when I was being pushed around, having to perform for people, that got a bit difficult. By November, I was just about finished."

He consulted his doctor, expecting to be ordered to rest. Instead he was referred to a cardiologist. "In no time I was in Ninewells Hospital, getting a pacemaker fitted. Since then, I've been all right."

Although his health has improved, his grief remains keen.

"Since I returned home, I've felt it more than I did when I was having to chase around and force myself. It's like being a rugby player. He only feels the pain of his bruises when the game is over."

Professor Whyte offered to drive me back to Leuchars railway station. As we passed the matchbox hotel by the Old Course, I asked him whether he played golf. Like a good St Andrean, he had tried. On occasions, he knocked the ball a respectable enough distance, but his shots had an unnerving habit of veering off to the right at the end of their flightpath.

"I was thinking as I got the car," he said, "that there was something we didn't discuss, didn't touch on at all."

"What was that?"

"We never talked about the 30 years I spent here teaching theology."

"Yes," I said, "the conversation did veer off a bit." Not, however, to the right.

Get Me Beltrami

JOSEPH BELTRAMI

Can you tell a lawyer by his waiting room? In Joseph Beltrami's, there is a large and splendidly ruinous red chair, as sore on an old lag's aching limbs as any High Court dock, and on the wall an odd collection of hangings: the Scottish Football League fixtures 1988-89; a poster advertising the satirical magazine, Private Eye; and, most curiously, a framed copy of the American Declaration of Independence.

I could hear Mr Beltrami in an adjoining office, booming out instructions to his assistants. Scotland's best-known criminal lawyer has a bass voice of intimidating timbre and range; he sounds like a dominie of that disciplinarian breed which vanished with the coming of guidance departments and the abolition of the belt. This impression was confirmed by his appearance in the open doorway. "Mr Kenneth Roy," he commanded. "Come this way please." He stands several inches above six feet and has the build of a heavyweight boxer a little past fighting best.

I thought I might get around to the mystery of the awful chair, and the other interesting distractions of the waiting room.

"I wondered about the poster in there. You read Private Eye?"

"No," he replied dismissively, as if I had asked a pretty silly question, which indeed I had. "But my wife Delia does."

Like a coward, I let it go at that.

★ ★ ★

Mr Beltrami's office is on the fifth floor of a block in West Nile Street, Glasgow, next door to a "cafe bar" and opposite Irvine Rusk the fashionable hairdresser. How out of place they must feel, those clients who remember the good old days before Glasgow became a self-conscious city of European culture — the golden era when Pat Roller of the Daily Record scoured the streets looking for trouble, Lord Carmont meted out condign punishment at the High Court, and Jimmy Boyle was just another baby-faced razor slasher.

Mr Beltrami himself is part of that old Glasgow. He was brought up at No. 132 The Briggate — a poor tenement district which has reluctantly bowed to the onward march of upwardly mobile cafe bar proprietors. His father, who was Swiss, ran a fish and chip shop (the Swiss Restaurant) at Glasgow Cross.

"A very hard-working man. Not well educated at all. Spent most of his time in the shop, peeling potatoes or serving. Worked six days a week, very long hours. He'd normally get home about midnight."

"So you didn't see much of him?"

"I saw much more of my mother. She decided to send me to a private school at the age of eight. St Aloysius College. I was the only child in the district who went there."

"Were you a happy child?"

"I had unhappy moments. I had to go to school each morning suitably attired. Blazer and cap, regulation trousers and socks. That caused a lot of problems. People made remarks."

"What sort of remarks?"

"'You're a cissy'. Remarks like that. I was very much out of place."

"What effect did that have on you?"

"It made me quite determined."

A boy in Stockwell Street called Cryans — Mr Beltrami spelled out the letters of his name — was the chief offender. Morning and night for two years, Cryans hurled obscenities at the nice lad in the blazer and cap until finally, provoked beyond endurance, young Joe challenged him to a fight, jackets off. "I hammered him," he said. "He never bothered me again."

"Were you interested in crime or the law?"

"No interest whatsoever. I had no relation in the law. I had no relation in the professions at all."

When he announced at St Aloysius that he wanted to be an

engine driver, his teacher ridiculed him and the rest of the class laughed with the particular cruelty of children. Joe Beltrami decided then to take refuge in the conventional ambitions of the well-educated. He would teach. He was still unenthusiastically committed to teaching as he boarded a tram at Charing Cross on his way to matriculate at Glasgow University. Then he met a chum.

"Don't be a fool," his friend said. "The Legal Aid Act's just come out. Law's the profession now. I'm going up to matriculate in law." By the time the tram reached Gilmorehill, so was Joe.

"What happened to your friend?"

"Gave up after six months. No application."

"Would you have enjoyed teaching?"

"I would have been bored to death. I wouldn't have had the patience for teaching."

"But you enjoy the law?"

"I find it thrilling. I've been doing it for more than 30 years, but I still feel the adrenalin. I've just finished a jury trial today. Finished an hour ago."

"Who won?"

"I got a unanimous not guilty. Good fighting case. The fiscal thought he had a good case, I thought he hadn't, and the jury agreed with me. It was a self-defence situation in Blantyre."

A self-defence situation in Blantyre. The mind boggled.

I first encountered Joe Beltrami when I was 19, and the Glasgow Herald's eager representative in the High Court. From a hard bench a few feet from the dock, I observed an endless succession of Glasgow CID men with Burton suits and matching stories point incriminatingly at Mr Beltrami's clients. I sat so close to these clients that, during a long trial, if the Glasgow CID men became more than usually boring, I could watch the hair grow on the back of the accused's neck.

In the dock was a trapdoor leading to the cells. At the end of a trial, if the verdict was guilty, two burly prison officers would pull open the trapdoor and bundle the convicted man down into the abyss. Over the months I spent there, a number of Mr Beltrami's clients went that unhappy route. But it was also noticeable how many emerged into the sunlight, to the bosoms of their families and the blandishments of the Scottish Daily Express. Of course, I was too awe struck actually to speak to Mr Beltrami. He was in any case usually deep in conversation with his learned counsel, a young dandy called Nicholas Fairbairn. Mr Fairbairn moved on to higher things, and in due course a knighthood; but Mr Beltrami, staying close to his roots, continued to present a good fighting case, and does so to this day.

"Does the criminal mind interest you?"

"I have been trying to fathom what goes on in the criminal mind for many years, and find it extremely difficult. It can be fascinating, but I'm puzzled by quite a number of my clients."

"Why?"

"Well, their reactions. I mean, I've had clients who're never out of the office prior to the trial. You do a lot of work for them, you go down there, you get them off, and at the end of the day, they just walk away. You'd expect them to be over the moon. I would be. But it's as if they fully expected it. They disappear quite nonchalantly."

"Is there such a thing as a born criminal?"

"I think many criminals are brought up to it. I've known grandfathers, fathers and sons, all doing the same thing...shoplifting, housebreaking, whatever. Three generations, all following in each other's footsteps."

"When a client comes to see you, do you ask him if he did it?"

"I don't. I can't speak for other solicitors."

"So how do you go about it?"

"What I say is, 'How do you plead to this charge?'"

"Why don't you ask if he did it?"

"I'm only the agent. I might get a difficult answer. A wrong answer. A misleading answer. So I put the onus on him."

"What if you discover he's done it?"

"At a second or third meeting, a client might say, 'Look, I haven't told you the whole truth. I was involved. I really did do this.' In that situation, I can do one of two things. Continue to act for him at the trial, without putting forward a substantive defence. In other words, I can test the prosecution case, challenge the prosecution to prove the charge beyond reasonable doubt. That's one option. Or I can advise the client to go elsewhere, consult another solicitor. I would tell him why I was doing that, so that he wouldn't make the same mistake again perhaps."

"Have you ever been frightened by a client?"

It seemed at first glance a superfluous question to put to Joseph Beltrami, who'd seen off the holy terror of Stockwell Street and could never have looked remotely like a cissy, even in a St Aloysius cap. But as I remembered the hairs growing at the back of some terrifyingly thick necks in the High Court, I asked him all the same...

"I've had clients here who've wanted me to do something that I didn't think was appropriate, something improper even. Trying to be too fly, as some of them tend to be, you know? Then I've had to say, 'I'm in charge of your case, I make the decisions, and if you're not happy about that, you can go elsewhere.' I will not be manipulated by a client. Never have been, never will be. So, yes, there have been words. Angry words."

But only words. Cryans remains the one protagonist of Mr Beltrami who has ever been asked to remove his jacket for what used to be known in Glasgow as a square go.

"This shot of adrenalin you get from handling criminal trials. What's that all about?"

"Excitement."

"You're excited by the uncertainty, perhaps?"

"Yes. You don't know the outcome of a case until the jury returns. You don't know whether your argument has been accepted. You don't know how receptive they'll be."

All around the walls of his office are black and white photographs of charitable and social occasions, and of various celebrities he has met. It could be a theatrical agent's office or perhaps a sporting promoter's; it doesn't look much like a Scottish solicitor's. Of course, Mr Beltrami is now something of a celebrity himself. But is he really an actor manque?

"I think many lawyers are actors."

"Are you?"

"To some extent, I am, yes."

"In what way?"

"Take the case I had today. Father and son charged with seriously assaulting some difficult chap in Blantyre."

Ah, yes. The self-defence situation in Blantyre.

"The father was supposed to have hit him with a stick, then the son came to the father's assistance and hit him with a golf club. They're both charged. Today, the father gave his evidence and told me exactly what he'd told me from the beginning — that he was trying to defend himself. But when I called the son, his story was that he saw his father being attacked, grabbed the golf club, gave the golf club to his father, and it was his father who hit the chap over the head with it. This was not what the son had told me beforehand. Lo and behold, my case falls apart at the seams. But I can't disclose that to the jury. Though the evidence of the son is very much against me, I have to look as if I am fairly satisfied."

"Do juries notice things like the defence lawyer's facial expression?"

"The jury's watching you even when you're just sitting taking notes. I'm always conscious of the fact that if a bad piece of evidence comes out, they'll look over at you. Well, you can't react with an ashen face, you can't give the impression that the ball's on the slates. Even when your position is getting worse and worse, you've got to look as if you can take it in your stride. Act buoyant. Smile if necessary."

"Have juries changed over the years?"

"No. I find juries fairly accurate on the whole. They generally come to the right decision, though not always by the proper means."

However, Mr Beltrami's confidence in Scots law is much diminished. He was a great admirer of our legal system until about 10 years ago. Then, he says, it began to be eroded in various ways. When I asked him how, he said that would take a great deal of time to explain and referred me to an article he had written for a legal journal. When I pressed him for an example to be going on with, he spoke vehemently about the law of corroboration.

"Ten years ago, before anyone could be convicted of a crime, there had to be two separate pieces of evidence pointing unequivocally at the accused. We used to call them two strong fingers of evidence. Not one. One witness was never sufficient, even if that witness was the Pope or the Moderator. There had to be proper, cogent corroboration. But we're now at the stage, remarkably and dramatically at times, when one man — the evidence of one person — can virtually convict someone. That's a very serious state of affairs."

"How upset are you when a client you believe to be innocent is found guilty. Does that get to you?"

"It shouldn't. The ideal is to be clinical. Detached. To be able to turn yourself off like a tap when the case is finished, and say, 'Well, I did my best.' But, in fact, we're all human."

That was Mr Beltrami's prompt to talk about his most celebrated client, Patrick Meehan, a Glasgow criminal who, wrongly convicted of murder, was freed after a tenacious campaign and granted the Royal Pardon — the first this century in a murder case. Above the desk is a photograph of Patrick Meehan receiving a cheque for £52,000 — the price for seven years' wrongful imprisonment.

"You were always convinced of Meehan's innocence?"

"Utterly. I take a certain pride in my judgement, my assessment of people, and I never thought for one moment that he could mislead me throughout the preparation of his case. The day he was convicted in Edinburgh, I came back to Glasgow by car, absolutely shattered — finished. For years afterwards, that case was on my mind."

When Joseph Beltrami began his career, a client wrongly convicted of murder would not have received a cheque for £52,000. He would have hanged.

"Have you known people who were hanged?"

"I've had 12 capital murder cases, but no one was executed. They were either acquitted, or convicted of lesser charges. But as a student, I went to the High Court several times to see capital murder trials, including the well-known case of Police Constable Robertson, the points policeman at Gorbals Cross, who drove over his girl friend in Prospecthill Road, then reversed back. I saw him give evidence, heard him being sentenced to death. He did hang."

"What were your feelings about that trial?"

"I found all capital cases extremely exciting. The adrenalin was there. You could hear a pin drop in a capital trial. Since the abolition of capital punishment, I've been in murder cases where the accused — 17 and 18 year olds, three or four together in the dock — have exchanged a joke. That never happened in capital cases. The accused knew full well that his life was in the balance.

No laughter then."

"And you found that exciting?"

"Extremely exciting. And entirely different from the type of murder trial one has now."

"What's lacking?" I might have added, "Apart from the black cap, of course."

"Well, atmosphere. A bit of atmosphere. In capital cases, the courts were packed. Remember the Walter Ellis case in '61? Half a mile queue outside the court. Peter Manuel in '58? A mile queue. Now you get two spectators in court for murder cases in the High Court. Just not the same interest."

I was left to reflect on the sad decline of the Glasgow murder trial, an institution which seems to have suffered the same spectacular loss of spectator appeal as the Glasgow music hall, where many other well-known acts also died a terrible death, though not, I understand, at the end of a judicially approved rope.

Mr Beltrami said that tomorrow, he was going to Forfar. It seemed a bit of a let down after the heady recollections of glory days in Glasgow High Court. But it would be another good fighting case, no doubt. And I left knowing that if ever I found myself involved in a self-defence situation in Blantyre, I would sling my 5-iron back in the bag, grab the nearest telephone and demand: "Get me Beltrami!"

Climb Every Mountain

JOHN SMITH

Among the videos stacked behind the television set in the Shadow Chancellor's sitting room are such screen hits as Octupussy, Casablanca, Watership Down and Local Hero, as well as an underrated short entitled John Smith's Party Election Broadcast 1983 (10 mins). Perched on the edge of the collection is a more recent addition — a Health Education cassette on coronary heart disease.

It is a bright, softly furnished room with lots of contemporary paintings, newspapers and books. The books, mostly political memoirs, are piled on a table against the wall.

"He's out," said one of Mr Smith's daughters, "but he won't be long. Would you like a coffee?"

When he arrived a few minutes later, he was carrying a shopping bag. "There's a guy from the BBC keeps 'phoning," he said. "Do you mind if I 'phone him back?" The papers were full of gloomy economic news; the £ was having another bad week, interest rates were on the march. He had been up at the crack of dawn to do an interview about it for breakfast television. Now Radio 4's The World Tonight wanted him back in the Edinburgh studio that evening. And this was John Smith on holiday, trying to relax during a Parliamentary recess.

For someone so recently at death's door, he looked almost offensively well. I must have said something to that effect, for he talked keenly about his pursuit of fitness since the heart attack which almost killed him.

"I really went at the business of getting fit with fanatical determination. I was storming about here doing five miles a day, climbing hills, all sorts of things."

"And now?", I asked anxiously, thinking about all those BBC interviews.

"Oh, I've begun to collect Munros," he said. "I climbed two only last Sunday. I walk with a group called the Rambling Radicals."

"Talking politics on the hoof?"

"Something like that."

"Would it have upset you very much if you'd had to chuck politics?"

"A heart attack is such a knock-out blow, especially after the initial euphoria of survival, and you're lying alone in the hospital wondering whether you're going to end up as a cardiac cripple. So yes, I did a lot of hard thinking. But funnily enough, the thought of coming out of politics wasn't too shattering. I mean, if I couldn't do it, I couldn't do it. I decided that I would accept the verdict and do what was sensible in the circumstances."

"What would you have done instead?"

"Gone back to the Bar. If I was able."

Even as a boy in the Argyllshire village of Ardrishaig, John Smith always wanted to be an advocate. When I asked him what took him into politics, he replied that he had often wondered that himself. He agreed that a West Highland schoolhouse was a somewhat unusual background for a Labour politician.

"But there was a political atmosphere in the house," he added on reflection. "I suppose you could call it a Christian socialist background. Not uncommon in the West Highlands."

"Tell me about your father. He was the village schoolmaster?"

"He was a shy, retiring sort of man. Quite different from me...I'm pretty extrovert. He had a strong sense of moral propriety, and a slight intellectual snobbery about people engaged in less worthy occupations than teaching."

"What did he think of your ambition to be a lawyer?"

"He looked at me as if to say, 'Well, if that's what the boy wants, I suppose it will do, but it's not as important as being a teacher.' That commitment to teaching was very important to him."

"Does the greatly diminished social status of the teacher trouble you?"

"I think it's a tragedy that teachers are not held in more esteem in the community. It is in many ways the crucial job."

At the age of 12, he went to Dunoon Grammar School as a boarder. One of his teachers was the novelist Robin Jenkins. It was there that he joined the young socialists — "I knew that was my side, somehow" — and the notion of political activity entered his head for the first time. He did a history degree at Glasgow University, before studying law for three years.

"They had this idea that you should get educated properly in the arts before you went into the law. That was an old Scottish tradition, and I'm very sad that it's passed from us."

"Because the law is too narrow a foundation?"

"It's a good mind-stretcher. It teaches analytical reasoning. But it doesn't stress imagination, it doesn't give you historical background or literary experience. You get people now going straight from school into the law of contract. That's a mature concept to grapple with at the age of 18."

At Glasgow, he joined a team of brilliant university debaters, which also included his friend and fellow socialist James Gordon, now managing director of Radio Clyde, who, had he pursued a political career, might today have been as incisive and convincing a Labour spokesman as John Smith himself.

"Are the qualities required to be a good lawyer essentially different from a politician's skills?"

"I'm the wrong person to answer that, because I think I use the techniques of the lawyer in politics. I try to be a rational person, constructing the argument and going through the stages of reasoning to come to a conclusion. I suppose I'm a bit guilty of cross-examining people, of attacking the government in a prosecutorial style."

This reminded me of Mr Smith's finest Parliamentary moment: his devastating indictment of the government at the height of the Westland crisis, that rum, forgotten scandal, which baffled the public but so excited the politicians that Mr Michael Heseltine strutted out of the Cabinet and Mrs Thatcher came close to being toppled.

"You use forensic skills. Does that mean you aren't at home with political rhetoric?"

"I mistrust political rhetoric," he said briskly.

"The Nye Bevan approach?"

"Oh, I don't know if that's fair. Nye Bevan was much more reasoned than some people give him credit for. As a matter of fact, if you read In Place of Fear, it's a tremendously moderate book. Advocating the mixed economy, for example. But I do mistrust political rhetoric, and I'm not a political revolutionary. Quite the opposite."

"What do you believe in?"

"I believe in steady progress. I'm the type of politician who wants to see things done. Houses built, schools opened, improvements made. A case of getting on with the work."

Mr Smith, unlike many in the Labour Party, actually finds opposition deeply frustrating. He is not one of socialism's natural soul-searchers. But I was beginning to wonder whether his proclamation of efficiency might be rather bloodless. Didn't he think that emotion played any part in politics?

"Oh, I think emotion is very important, in the sense that the basic political instincts — justice, fair treatment, compassion — are moral. But what I've got to do, it seems to me, is not to preach about it, but to get it done. That's my task in the chain, as it were. Other people might have the brilliant idea, the illuminating moral concept, and that's a very legitimate role. It's not me, that's all."

When he was 22, and still a law student, he was invited by Douglas Young, late Professor of Classics at St Andrews, who ran the local Labour Party, to fight the (then) safe Conservative seat of East Fife in a by-election.

"Half of Glasgow University decamped to the constituency. Some of them weren't even members of the Labour Party, but there was this tremendous sense of being 'their man'. I managed to beat the Liberal by 90 votes, which wasn't bad considering that it subsequently became a Liberal seat."

Later, he turned down the chance of contesting a more winnable seat in Aberdeen. As he now candidly volunteers, the idea of representing a marginal constituency, with all its attendant insecurities, was not attractive. Instead he completed his legal training and as a newly qualified solicitor endured a baptism of fire: night lawyer on the Sunday Mail. In this capacity, he advised the notoriously volatile editor, Sandy Webster, on the libel risks associated with the paper's frank and fearless exposes of swindling West of Scotland car dealers. He was called to the Scottish Bar, with some relief doubtless, in 1967.

His cautiousness paid off: in 1970, the year of Mr Heath's unexpected victory at the polls, he was selected for one of Labour's Lanarkshire strongholds. After only a year at Westminster, he fell out with his party over Europe, defying a three-line whip, and found himself in the doghouse. The experience, though it did him no harm, confirmed what he had all along suspected: that it was important in politics to have a proper job to go back to.

"How has Parliament changed in the last 20 years?"

"The quality of the members has gone up a great deal, especially in Scotland. I notice it more on my own side, but it may be true of other parties. We've certainly got the best intake we've ever had in the Labour Party in Scotland. There are young, able, committed people coming in, people of real distinction in other jobs. But I'm getting tired of the impotence of Parliament. This period of Thatcher government has revealed Parliament's weakness in relation to the executive. It greatly needs strengthened."

"What do you think of the new Conservatism?"

For the first time in our talk, Mr Smith's amiability deserted him.

"Dislike it intensely," he said with feeling. "I regard it as vulgar, unprincipled, almost immoral. This notion that the individual must look after himself."

"Why is that immoral?"

"Because," he said — and now he might have been back in the West Highland schoolhouse of his childhood — "you must care for others. People have selfish instincts, and unselfish instincts. I take on the whole an optimistic view of humanity. I think when the chips are down, people are good rather than bad, but you must always be reinforcing the good, appealing to it, developing it. When she said there was no such thing as society, only individuals and families, that seemed to me such a barren philosophy. I find it hard to agree with someone who believes that the point of the Good Samaritan is that he had money to help the person in need."

"What's your reading of the parable?"

"Just that you help someone who IS in need. Some walk by on the other side, the Good Samaritan didn't. That was why he was good. It so happened he had money to pay for the person's upkeep."

Mr Smith sat forward eagerly on the sofa, and talked in an animated way about why he so disliked the Prime Minister. There were, he thought, many Conservative MPs who also disliked her, but who kept quiet because of her authoritarian management of the party.

"I didn't expect you to approve of her," I said when the splendid tirade was over, "but I wondered whether you might secretly admire some of her political qualities."

"Anybody who wins three general elections is a formidable political operator. I recognise that. I recognise that she's got natural authority and courage, that she's very spirited, pretty determined, almost ruthless. Well, she is ruthless. But while I recognise all these things, I don't have to admire her or approve of her policies."

"I notice that you don't list honesty among her attributes. Yet she does have this popular reputation as a straight from the shoulder operator, doesn't she?"

"I wouldn't rate her particularly honest. I wouldn't say she was dishonest. I think she's a pretty tricky politician, frankly."

"Do you think that any top politician can be totally honest?"

"It's difficult," he sighed, "to conduct politics in the glare of publicity. You must never tell lies, I'm clear about that. But it's how far you reveal what you know." I asked for an example. Well, say you had decided on a policy, but the timing of its announcement was critical. Meanwhile, somebody asked you about it, and a temporising answer wouldn't do. Then what? Yes, he thought, that was a problem. But it was important to understand that the House of Commons was a forgiving place — a wild place, but a forgiving one. If you had something to apologise for, the best course was to put it right as soon as you could. If you didn't, they would stalk you for months.

"Mrs Thatcher seems to have tapped a conservative instinct in many of Labour's natural supporters. That's an odd phenomenon."

"Hmmm."

"Hasn't it cost you three elections?"

"It has. Mind you, I think the Labour Party had itself to blame for quite a lot of what went wrong." There followed a brief analysis of Labour's internecine warfare in the early Eighties and Mrs

Thatcher's apparently boundless good fortune, all the way from the Falklands Factor to the North Sea Oil Bonanza.

"But just getting back to this conservative instinct in the traditional working-class Labour supporter..."

"Yes, many working people are socially conservative."

"And she's given them their council houses. They've really done rather well out of 10 years of Mrs Thatcher?"

"I don't fully understand this. It's not a phenomenon I've noticed much in Scotland. If people in my constituency choose to buy their council house, they don't on the whole change their vote as a result."

I noticed that the book on top of the pile was Roy Jenkins's biography of Stanley Baldwin. Were there any Conservative politicians he admired? He said he had some time for Mr Heath, whom he judged crusading and honourable though lacking in political skills, and Alick Buchanan-Smith, the Kincardine MP, who had resigned on an issue of principle and had since maintained a dignified opposition.

"And R.A. Butler. I never had any dealings with him, but I've read a lot about him."

"You admired him, perhaps, because he was a humane Conservative?"

"Yes, that's the strand in Conservatism I like. Oddly enough, I find that their aristocratic wing is more attractive. They have a more genuine sense of public service. What you get on the Conservative benches now are jumped-up estate agents and failed unit-trust men."

"What about political heroes on your own side?"

There was a pause. "I don't go in for heroes very much" was his surprising answer. "But I think history will regard Attlee as a tremendously capable and effective politician, very much of the pragmatic type. He didn't lead anybody to the barricades, but there's no doubt about it, he held a talented government together extremely well, and made tremendous changes. Freedom for India. The welfare state in Britain. He will go down as a colossus of the 20th century. Among people I know well, I've a lot of affection for Jim Callaghan."

A lurch of memory was required to bring Labour's last Prime Minister — in whose Cabinet John Smith served as Trade Secretary — back into sharp focus.

"He's a forgotten man," I said.

"Yes, and that's a bit unfair. He blossomed when he became Prime Minister, he was much better at that than as Foreign Secretary. But he didn't have a proper run at being Prime Minister. I liked his style. He was a decent man, Jim. So different from Thatcher. In his Cabinet, you could speak up, advance a view. No inhibition at all on making a case."

"Wasn't he a bit of a trimmer? He admitted as much."

"Oh, Jim was a very adroit politician. Bit over-cautious and conservative."

"Do you need to trim in order to be a Labour leader?"

Mr Smith's reply was uncharacteristically hesitant. "I think all politicians have a sense of positioning," he said carefully. "Trimming...Well, it's not so much that. But there are times when you can spoil a case by arguing it too vigorously."

Like nuclear disarmament? Hadn't Labour been trimming madly on that?

"Yes, well, I agree very much with the policy review, which means that I had reservations about the policy prior to that. But I loyally put it forward. If that's trimming, then trimming is necessary, because if we all go firing in individual directions, you'll have no political party. A party has to have a discipline. If it's such a big issue for you, you resign. A politician must always leave that door open for himself if he feels he can't serve with honour."

Now that Labour had ditched unilateralism and the word nationalisation was studiously avoided, I suggested that there was little in the party's policies to which any reasonable man could object. Where was the socialism?

Peering benignly over his spectacles, Mr Smith objected to my implicit assumption that a reasonable man would find socialism objectionable. There was, he went on, a good deal of socialism in the policy review. He then reeled off a number of tax and social security proposals which he called socialist. When I persisted that these sounded like social welfare objectives rather than socialist, he said he saw no distinction. He instructed me a little on the nature of market systems, which were either value-neutral or value-hostile.

"My model," he concluded, "is Sweden. It is a very good example of two ambitions I have — to see a strong economy and a fair society. I happen to think at this stage in our development, we should be able to have both."

"Isn't that the only socialist economy in the world which has actually worked consistently?"

"Well, Austria's had quite a lot of success. The situation in Europe is complicated by coalitions. What is quite clear is that right-wing Thatcherism hasn't crossed the English Channel."

I was still thinking about James Callaghan. It occurred to me that John Smith must be one of the very few members of the Shadow Cabinet who had served at a senior level in the Callaghan government. Wasn't Labour's lack of political experience a handicap?

"I'm one of two ex-Cabinet ministers in the Shadow Cabinet," he confirmed. (The other is Roy Hattersley.) "But there are others who were knocking on the door of the Cabinet. The difference between being a senior minister of state and the boss of a department isn't an enormous one. And experience isn't everything. It's a curious thing about government. You learn it very quickly."

"Do you want to be Prime Minister one day?"

"I'm not bothered about it," he said. "I would very much like to be Chancellor of the Exchequer and hold a senior position in the government. But I don't have this driving power urge that politicians seem to have. I'm very careful about not making all of my life political. I think you've got to have other interests."

This seemed a suitable moment to return briefly to the subject of Mr Smith's heart attack.

"Even if you were philosophical about the possibility of losing your political career — didn't you have any dark nights of the soul?"

"It was a bit of crisis, there's no doubt about that. But I knew I was going to survive...well, I sort of believed I would survive. I was really just thankful that I was there at all...grateful for small mercies, you know?"

"Did you think about death?"

"Well, I'm a Christian. If anything, what happened confirmed my faith. But not in any dramatic way."

"Do you consciously interpret politics in a Christian way?"

"I'm not arrogant or foolish enough to argue that you can't be a Conservative and a good Christian. Whether you have a mixed economy or a state economy...this is to some extent a matter of judgement. But people who argue that poverty should be tolerated or even encouraged — as some American right-wingers do — are stepping over the line. So I divide political issues into those that are sharply moral and those that are more matters of judgement and tactics. In that sense, I suppose I have inherited my father's Christian socialism."

We had come full circle.

On my way out, we paused before an impressive photograph of the last Labour Cabinet. There in the front row was a young, unsmiling Dr David Owen; there, too, such forgotten luminaries as Roy Mason. How few of the faces suggested names. "So many have gone," Mr Smith said softly. "Quite frightening, really."

Two years from now, the picture may look quite different. By then, Labour may be back, this immensely able and likeable politician may be Chancellor of the Exchequer, and a more cheerful portrait may be hanging in the hall of his family home. Mr Smith may also have bagged a complete set of Munros.

The Honorary Trusty

JEAN MORRIS

"Tell me about your first time in prison."

"I remember hearing the gate close behind me, walking down to the hall, putting my hand out to open the door into the corridor, and realising there wasn't a handle. Suddenly, keys were the be all and end all of life."

"Were you frightened?"

"No, but that was probably my stupidity."

Since then, Jean Morris has spent the best part of 30 years in and out of prison. Chairman of the Scottish Parole Board for the length of an average life sentence, she is such a familiar figure in our jails that she should be made an honorary trusty.

When I met her, they had let her out for the day. We faced each other across a pretty room in the Glasgow Cathedral manse, and in this incongruous setting discussed such matters as slopping out and other disgraces of our penal system. She looks and sounds like one of those humane, indomitable Scotswomen who subscribe to an old-fashioned concept of service to the community. With her energy and intelligence, she might have ended up running any one of a hundred voluntary organisations for the deserving poor or disadvantaged. Instead she has chosen to devote her life to society's offenders.

"How did it come about?"

Her husband Dr William Morris (minister of Glasgow Cathedral, and one of the drier wits in the Church of Scotland) had been minister of Peterhead at the time, and Mrs Morris — agitated about the housing shortage in the town — had got herself elected to the local council.

"As a magistrate, I became a visitor to the prison. Then Bill was made chaplain. He came home one night and said, 'Look, there's nothing for the prisoners, but there is a beautiful stage. Why don't I speak to the governor and see if he'll allow you to do three one-act plays with some of the long-term men?' And the governor said, 'Of course — if she's daft enough.' So I went ahead."

"What were the plays?"

"I can't remember their names, but I do remember one was set in a golf clubhouse, frightfully pukka, Muirfield sort of place. There was a body involved, and I had an awful job getting somebody to play the body, because he had to lie there motionless for half an hour."

Eventually, one Jake McCurdy, a diminutive Glasgow hard man, came to the rescue. Mr McCurdy, who has subsequently departed to that great open prison in the sky, appears to have been relatively charming as armed robbers go. Mrs Morris, employing her incidental talent for mimicry, gave the following account of his audition:

'I could do it, miss. I'm no good at learning lines, but I could do it.'

'But Jake, you'd have to lie still.'

'Oh, I can lie still for hours on end.'

'What are you in for, Jake?'

'I held up a post office in Paisley, miss.'

'With a real gun?'

'Of course wi' a real gun!' Jake said indignantly. 'Whit did ye expect?'

Jake was admirably cast: he could indeed lie still for hours on end. But some members of the company were not so proficient. Mrs Morris had to work hard at encouraging the Peterhead thespians to give expression and emphasis to their lines. It is the same with amateur actors the world over.

"One of the key lines in the play was, 'My goodness, you don't see a dead body every day.' I said to the guy, 'Dammit all, you can't just come in and say it like that. I mean, you DON'T see a dead body every day, do you?' And a voice from the wings piped up, 'Who's kiddin' who, miss?'"

During rehearsals, she was left alone with 10 convicted

murderers. The only actor who refused to learn his lines was a particularly lethal character called Larry Winters.

"How did you cope with him?"

"Eventually by ordering him off the stage and back to his cell, forgetting of course that I had no officer there to enforce the instruction. There was a pregnant moment when he just stood there on the stage, and in that one moment, fear engulfed me. I was suddenly aware that it was a case of my personality and his, and that if mine didn't win, I was a dead duck. Well, finally he shrugged his shoulders and jumped off the stage, went up to the door and rang the bell. When we finished that night, one of the others, a double murderer, said to me, 'Never you do that again. Never. If one of us back stage had supported Winters, there's nothing the rest of us could have done about it.'"

Later, Mr Winters was transferred to Barlinnie Prison in Glasgow, where he hanged himself.

"Need prisons be such appalling places?"

"Absolutely not. Prison is basically how men are treated. It's not really so much to do with things like slopping out as with human relationships. Prisoners will tell you that if you can produce a regime which is fair, and where nine tenths of the prisoners are prepared to work alongside the staff if not entirely with them, then the last tenth doesn't matter, and you won't have rooftop demonstrations."

"But we do have rooftop demonstrations, and worse. Are you saying that the regime isn't fair?"

"A jail has to be run with the goodwill of its prisoners. But if officers are not prepared to accept that prisoners are people, if they regard them as scum, then you're in for trouble. The officers can never win, they're so much in the minority."

"So you think that staff attitudes are at the root of the problems in our prisons?"

"Oh, yes. Absolutely. I would rather see the money spent on retraining every single prison officer, than in putting a toilet in every cell."

"Is the wrong type of person becoming a prison officer?"

"Not becoming, but has become in the past. They've taken in two or three hundred new officers in this past year, but they're vastly outnumbered by chaps who've been there 10, 15, 20 years, and those are still the ones who rule the prisons."

Despite the depressingly repressive nature of the regime, Mrs Morris remains optimistic about the potential for rehabilitation ("I believe in it, I have seen it happen") and encouraged by the achievements of the Barlinnie Special Unit for disruptive long-term prisoners. But when I mentioned the unit's former star pupil, the well-known sculptor and author Jimmy Boyle, her enthusiasm was subdued.

"The professional in me hopes that Jimmy Boyle is what he appears to be — a complete success. I wouldn't give the credit entirely to the Special Unit. There is also the fact that he married money, and was lifted into a different world. And he certainly had an awful lot of important people supporting him, including people in your own profession."

"You will agree he hasn't offended again, and appears to be leading a blameless life?"

"Oh, I don't think Jimmy will revert to the Jimmy of bygone years, I really don't. I have a feeling that he is not as sincere a person as I would like him to be, but then I think probably I would like him to be a saint, and I'm not a saint, nor are you, so why should I expect Jimmy Boyle to be a saint?"

She had spoken more warmly of Jake McCurdy.

Not only is Jean Morris a wife of the manse; she is also a daugher of one. Her father, the Reverend D.P. Howie, was minister of Laigh Kirk, Kilmarnock, for half a century.

At the age of eight, Jean was a keen athlete and liked to compete against children several years her senior. Then one day she went fishing for baggy minnows in a river near the manse. The doctors suggested that was how she might have picked up the bug.

"If I was going to get polio at all," she said, "I was glad to get it so soon. You have less to give up. Later in life, it's much harder to bear. When I was young, it never struck me that I was different from anybody else. I remember having splints up to my shoulder, and a girl saying to me, 'When are you going to be better, Jean?'. 'Better?' I said. 'But I am better.' I could run around in my splints almost as fast as she could. And I had a mother and a housekeeper who never let me believe that I was different or even that I was ill."

"You were off school for a long time?"

"Two years. I had to teach myself to read, really educate myself with a bit of help from visiting teachers."

"Did that make you a lonely child?"

"Not at all. I always had kids from the neighbourhood who came in to play. Though not perhaps for the first six or seven months, when I was pretty well immobile. I lay on a bed in the outer wing of the manse. My mother gave me a badminton racquet and a shuttle, and I played this off against the wall. I suppose my mother must have broken her heart over it — her only child struck down by polio — but I was never allowed to feel sorry for myself. Mother was a quite remarkable woman. Look, there she is at 18, just behind you..."

Mrs Morris pointed to a painting of a strikingly lovely girl.

"Isn't it a beautiful portrait?" she said with feeling. "It was done by a man called Greig, an Aberdeen artist. He was killed a few months later in a train accident. Mother was an artist, too."

"Did she enjoy being a minister's wife?"

"People said she was the most unlikely minister's wife. But I don't think she regretted becoming one. She was religiously very right-wing and would go to bed at night and tell my father to stop putting ideas into my head."

"What sort of ideas?"

"Father always said you had to question everything, think things out for yourself, if religion was to have any real meaning for you. I was questioning the virgin birth and the resurrection before the Bishop of Durham was ever heard of!"

"Are you still questioning them?"

"I've now reached the stage — I may have reached it many years ago — where the literal interpretation of both these events is quite unimportant. The important thing is that Christ lived and died and turned the world upside down by the impact of his personality."

"Are you saying that the resurrection doesn't matter? Isn't it at the centre of Christian belief?"

"I interpret it as resurrection of the spirit, the whole being that was Christianity, not necessarily that he might have resurrected as a body. What kind of body, I know not."

"How important is religion to you?"

"What is important to me is the idea of the fatherhood of God and therefore the brotherhood of man, and that is the idea that has motivated most of my life — the idea that we are here to see the needs of others and do what we can to help."

After winning a bursary competition for Glasgow University, Jean Howie realised that attending Gilmorehill would be physically too inhibiting. She was 17 and eager for independence. Instead she went to St Andrews, where she was able to cycle to and from lectures without assistance. She did famously there, winning a badminton blue, a classics degree, and the presidency of the union.

'You're far too interesting a person to become a blue stocking,' her Latin professor told her. 'What you want is to get into the world of philosophy and psychology.' With this encouragement, she did a second degree in educational psychology (with first-class honours), and began a career as a clinical psychologist at the Royal Hospital for Sick Children in Edinburgh.

"We ran a clinic. Every sort of behavioural problem and personality defect. Thieves, young prostitutes...you name it, we had it."

"You had come from a fairly sheltered background. How did all this hit you?"

Mrs Morris gave one of her jolly laughs.

"Oh, I went home one weekend and said to my mother, 'There is not one normal person or family in the whole of Edinburgh!'"

"Did this work stimulate an interest in the criminal mind — or had you always had an interest?"

"I'd never thought about the criminal mind until I started in Sick Kids. What interested me more were the conditions in which a lot of these children lived."

"Did you decide that the criminal is a product of his environment?"

"Partly, yes. But I was always intrigued by the family where you got the one bad guy and all the others were successful. I think there is something much deeper than the environment, something in the make-up of the personality."

"Not heredity?"

"A throwback, if you like. The fellow who is much more likely to be influenced by the negative factors in society. Aggression. Wanting to fight. Wanting to destroy and determined that that's the only way he can succeed. He doesn't bother learning at school:

that's boring. His mother's and father's advice: that's boring. He wants to get out and get the adrenalin running."

"Do you encounter that a lot in your prison work?"

"Very much so. I was at Castle Huntly the other day, chatting to some of the boys. In one or two of them, you see the beginnings of a realisation that maybe there is another way. Maybe. But there are others for whom nothing's any good. The family's rotten, the house is rotten, everything's rotten. 'I'll bash his face in when I get out' — that primitive, primitive level. And I find it terribly frightening. Well, perhaps not so much frightening…It is just the most depressing thing to hear. One despairs."

"Because it's not treatable?"

"It isn't. It's like a cancer that cannot be treated."

Parole is not universally popular, even among prisoners. Critics outside see it as going soft on criminals; critics inside are just as suspicious, but for different reasons. For 10 years now, Jean Morris has been fending off attacks on her board.

"Is it true that a lot of prisoners refuse to be considered for parole?"

"There are always prisoners who say, 'To hell with parole. When we get out of prison, we want to be free men.' Because if you get parole, you are on licence, under supervision, liable to recall. Parole is continuing your sentence in the community. That's what it really means."

"Can you understand the public's hostility to the idea of potentially dangerous criminals being released a third of the way through their sentence?"

"I think there's still a certain amount of public dismay when somebody who's serving say a nine-year sentence gets out after three. In fact, very few nine-year men do get out after three. They might get out after four or five. But that would be at the second or third time of asking."

"Do you think sentences are too long?"

"I don't think so. Some crimes are so horrendous that people have to be put away for a fairly long period as a punishment."

"What is the punishment, exactly?"

"The punishment is in the separation from the family."

"What about the death penalty? Would you bring it back?"

"Totally against. I think it's legalised murder. We don't have the right to take human life."

"An eye for an eye, a tooth for a tooth?"

"I don't believe in that," she said passionately. "I've got 378 life sentence prisoners out there in the community now, living good, honest, decent lives and if we'd had the death penalty, they'd all be in their graves."

From this brave, sensible woman, I had heard a statement to shame the hangers.

After Tribune

GUS MacDONALD

Many years ago, when Taggart was a young constable, the local acting fraternity had not yet taken the high road, and a newsreader called John Toye was one of Scotland's most familiar faces, I made my only appearance on Scottish Television. The programme was called Talking Heads. Three people — Cliff Hanley and Ruth Wishart were the other hired heads — agreed to sit on a sofa and chat for half an hour. "Make it lively," the director ordered us. "Make it spontaneous." These are always deeply dispiriting instructions. In the heat of the studio, surrounded by lethargic technicians, our painfully contrived spontaneity quickly foundered. We discovered we had nothing interesting to say about J.M. Barrie, or golf, or any of the other conversational hares which our chairman Mr Hanley bravely set hirpling. Afterwards, in the hospitality room, Miss Wishart sounded upset about our performance; I think she feared (wrongly, as it happened) that she had scuppered her chances of further guest appearances. We drowned our sorrows; the hospitality flowed as our talk had not.

I mention this only to show how much broadcasting in Scotland has changed. At that time, Scottish Television was a tame, provincial animal, a pantomime horse of an outfit. It made low-budget programmes for its own audience, and contributed almost nothing to the ITV network apart from a tartan pastiche on Hogmanay. Its status now is greatly improved. Its programmes are shown south of the border more often than before, and those made for purely local consumption are generally of a higher standard.

It is difficult to imagine the present Director of Programmes, Gus MacDonald, tolerating anything as shabby as Talking Heads. Since he returned to Scotland in 1986 after a distinguished career with Granada Television, he has become Scottish broadcasting's most dynamic ambassador. He is clearly destined for higher things.

He is not, however, the most punctual person I met on my travels among the great and the good of our small country. At the company's offices in Glasgow, I turned up at the hour stipulated by his press officer, Mr Jardine, and waited to be called. Fifteen minutes went by. Eventually, the commissionaire took pity on me and telephoned a second time.

I was taken to an airless ante-room containing a telly, a video, some Japanese film stock, and a cabinet full of Schweppes soda water. A Scottish Tourist Board book entitled The VIP Guide to Scotland — obviously not intended for me — lay on a table. Mr Jardine appeared with apologies, but no consoling refreshments — perhaps the hospitality budget is not what it was.

"He was in London all day yesterday," Mr Jardine said. "He's in a meeting now."

"Ah."

"He's a favourite pundit for interviews and profiles," Mr Jardine continued. "Would you like a picture?"

"Thanks, but that won't be necessary."

The conversation was beginning to remind me of dear old Talking Heads at its scintillating best. When it finally ran into the sand, he made his excuses and left. I could hear him on the telephone in the next room, discussing the autumn schedules.

Presently, he re-emerged looking mildly triumphant. "Gus will see you now," he declared, leading me down a narrow corridor lined with portraits of Scottish celebrities — some dead, others forgotten, a few both dead and forgotten.

"I hope you don't mind if I stay for the interview," he said pleasantly. "It's just that Gus usually likes someone to be there when he gives interviews."

"Not at all."

At the end of the corridor, I was shown into a room of startling decor. Everything appeared to be either black or red; mostly black. The Director of Programmes, a big, muscular man with a moustache, shook my hand vigorously and ushered me to a sofa. Mr MacDonald is a journalist who obeys a valuable dictum of his trade: never apologise, never explain. He said nothing about the fact that our programme was now 35 minutes behind its advertised time. Instead he promptly challenged me to sum up my book in a sentence.

"OK," he said, when I had accomplished this difficult task. "No high policy stuff on the future of television. Stephen, I don't think we'll be needing you."

Mr Jardine rose and left without a word. When he had gone, Mr MacDonald began talking, with extraordinary fluency and force, about the childhood influences which shaped his life.

He was born in the village of Larkhall. Most of the male members of the family on his mother's side were Lanarkshire miners with a strong tradition of support for the Independent Labour Party.

"It surprised me when I came back to Scotland to discover that Larkhall had gone from red to orange. It had always been at the centre of radical activity in the history of the Lanarkshire coalfields, and while there was an anti-Catholic tradition, rooted in the Calvinism of the Scottish Labour movement, it certainly never degenerated into the kind of sectarianism you see today."

"What's caused that?"

"It's a rather sad reflection on the change that can happen over a generation when you take away a fundamental industry like mining."

His father, who worked for the Clyde Trust ("the Highlanders' Navy"), came originally from Skye. His grandfather's house was one of the communal houses for Gaels arriving in Glasgow.

"Was your father political?"

"The only political organisation he claims he ever belonged to was the Young Imperialist League, because they had the best snooker table in Partick. But he was a regular reader of Tribune, which I was brought up on from a pretty early age. Almost as soon as I could read, I was introduced to politics and political literature. There was that auto-didactic, self-taught tradition you get in the Scottish working-class. The old, blind woman up the stair (by this time, the family had moved from Larkhall to the Kingston district of Glasgow — the Plantation) had all the books of Tom Paine, so they were supplied to me. To that extent, it was a very political upbringing."

"But not a religious one?"

"I was brought up as an atheist. But there was never a strong sense of hostility to the Church of Scotland in the way that someone of my background might have felt hostility to the Church of England, which was seen as the Tory Party on its knees. I was therefore sent along to Church twice on a Sunday, and was quite active in Church groups. And on street corners, I was involved in a constant debate about theology with my peers, who were mainly Catholics."

Church-going atheists; anti-Catholic socialists — I was receiving an interesting education on the philosophical quirks of the West of Scotland working-class. But hang about: how come anti-Catholicism was politically inspired?

"Because the Catholic Church was seen as reactionary and hierarchical. It had supported Franco in the Spanish Civil War, had supported Hitler in the early days. There was also the belief that the Irish were used to break the trade unions, especially in the coalfields of Lanarkshire in the 19th century and even in the shipyards later. So there was a progressive content to people's anti-Catholicism. But it was never in my experience racist."

He attended Scotland Street School before anyone had heard of its architect, Charlie Rennie Mackintosh; then won a scholarship to Allan Glen's, where he was a keen footballer. I forgot to ask which position he played, but I would be surprised if it was defensive.

"You left very young."

"I left at 14. It was a curious business. I enjoyed the sporting side, but I never felt that I fitted. It was as if I was older than the kids in caps and blazers. The boys I'd grown up with were much more street-wise and their way of life was more interesting and exciting than anything on offer at Allan Glen's. So the prospect of spending all these years taking Highers, and then going through a university in order to end up as a metallurgist in ICI, didn't appeal."

I thought of another poor Glasgow boy who won a scholarship to Allan Glen's and did become a metallurgist. But it is possible that Monty Finniston never played football.

"Did you live to regret not going on to university?"

"No, I didn't. I can see the romantic appeal of having gone to Oxford or Cambridge. I can see very little romantic appeal in having gone to a nine to five university like Glasgow or

Edinburgh."

"They won't like you for saying that."

"Well, Edinburgh maybe isn't, but Glasgow is. I'd also been to Strathclyde briefly for sandwich courses — it was the Royal College, then. It was full of kids singing rugby songs and pouring beer in each other's pockets. People that no self-respecting young Glasgow buck would want to be seen with."

Mr MacDonald sat bear-like at his desk, jacket off. His physical strength, forceful intelligence, quick wit and native arrogance make him an impressive figure. He is an unmistakable son of the West of Scotland. He is macho man with brains.

"So you went into the yards?"

"To Stephens shipyard. I'm told that in Stephens, the Catholics went into the black squads, and the Protestants became fitters and electricians. Billy Connolly believes that quite strongly. Anyway, I ended up as a fitter, and did a five-year apprenticeship."

"What did you think of the Clyde shipbuilders as a race?"

"It was exciting being in the yards, especially if you were a kid of 15 or 16. You were thrown into a very busy community of 3,000 men, many of whom were very funny, some of whom were very well read, all of whom seemed to be pretty argumentative. But you weren't very well trained. You just picked things up on the job."

"Did working there develop you politically?"

"The extraordinary thing was that there was very little political activity at that time. This was the mid-Fifties, probably the height of the Cold War period, and any kind of overt left-wing activity was very small indeed. It had gone underground, almost. There wouldn't be more than half a dozen you could call socialist activists."

"Were you one of them?"

"I used to sell Tribune in the yard. I'd sell maybe 24 copies at most. A lot of the chaps who bought it disagreed with me politically, but just enjoyed the argument. I remember one of the journeymen turners, wee Hughie. He was an existentialist, which meant that his activities were purely confined to greyhound racing. He refused to take part in any kind of organised trade union or political activity. Odd thing, though. We started a philosophical society."

He was still playing football a lot. He was also drinking hard, and going out with girls. He was a frequenter of Glasgow's many ballrooms (Locarno on a Friday). His reading suffered.

The yards began to wind down. He never forgot the shock when Barclay Curle closed; it was like being told that the Bank of Scotland had gone bust. With fewer ships to build, he did hardly any work. He spent the night shifts arguing the toss with Charlie Fraser, a journeyman just back from Greenwich Village. "Nobody bothered you too much. It was the last province of industrial anarchy."

At the end of his apprenticeship, he joined the exodus of talent to London. There he met and married a girl called Teen whose family ran Shoreditch Labour Party, and landed himself a job on his beloved Tribune as circulation manager. His two best salesmen were a Mr Kinnock and a Mr Sillars. He impressed the managing editor, Michael Foot, by increasing the circulation from 12,000 to 14,000.

"But that was a bad thing, because I'd decided I wanted to be a journalist. They reckoned they could find journalists anywhere — they were pouring out of the universities — but it was very hard to find circulation managers."

In left-wing media London, however, bright Scots get on. He was introduced to Harold Evans, the campaigning editor of the Sunday Times, who gave him freelance work, and to Magnus Magnusson, later of quiz show and ancient monuments fame, who was about to return to Scotland to run a new investigative feature in the Scotsman. He returned with him. Apparently Scotland in those days was blameless, or Messrs Magnusson and MacDonald were incurious: the feature was not a great success. But the experience did him no harm; he was promptly appointed editor of the paper's new financial supplement. He was 26, had been in journalism for a year, couldn't type, and felt insecure about his grammar. Could such a meteoric rise happen now in the same way?

"I think it was difficult for someone like myself without any qualifications to get in once the trade unions tried to professionalise the industry."

"You regret that?"

"I do. It's always something that's worried me, the mystique that trades try to build around themselves. They've been the keepers of their mysteries since medieval times, and that tradition continues. I was looking the other day at a closed-shop decree of London plumbers made in 1380, which was remarkably close to some of those you could have found in broadcasting not 10 years ago."

Mr MacDonald was beginning to sound less like the boy who once sold Tribune in Stephens shipyard. Then the precise nature of his antipathy became clear.

"When I saw university graduates pretending to be trade union militants, when I saw trade unionism deployed by social workers or professional people in television or journalism, I did find it a bit distasteful, because it can in the end become a conspiracy against the public good."

"What's wrong with middle-class trade unionism?"

"Trade unionism," he replied vigorously, "is a defensive strategy of the industrial working-class."

He moved quickly out of newspapers. Then, unlike now, most ambitious young journalists believed that the future lay in television rather than print. He joined Granada Television's "investigative bureau" in 1967, making his name as a brilliant producer on World in Action. He remained with the company for almost 20 years.

"Here was a new area of journalism opening up in television. Investigative journalism was high fashion at that time. Almost every newspaper in Fleet Street had what Private Eye called its grope squad."

"Yet it's hardly mentioned as a term now."

"Well, it's an expensive form of journalism. It needs a lot of commitment from a company, rigorous standards, and a lot of hard work from the journalists employed in it."

"Does it go on at all these days?"

"World in Action still practises it by the week, keeps banging away. And This Week, with Death on the Rock. It's also still alive and fairly well in the Observer."

"What gave you most satisfaction at World in Action?"

"We pushed the Poulson investigation strongly. We also conducted a whole series of investigations into torture and repression around the world, which has been credited with changing the climate in the 1970s and perhaps even influencing the Carter administration. And we were the first people to carry out a systematic investigation of the risks involved in nuclear energy."

How noble all that sounded, and how remote. World in Action may still be banging away, if not, alas, with the same energy or impact — but for how much longer? As the television ratings war intensifies, and de-regulation proceeds apace, opportunities for first-class journalism on television — indeed for first-class programmes of any kind — steadily diminish. The week we met, the government had announced that it would not relent on its earlier decision to put the ITV franchises up for auction. Mr MacDonald was depressed about that, as well he might be.

"Can you see yourself moving out of television?"

"I really don't know. There are so many uncertainties. It may well be that a new kind of television will come that I don't want to work for. A new kind of politically craven management, which doesn't see itself as having any commitment to journalism."

It struck me that, if he had followed the career route of his two best salesmen at Tribune, Mr MacDonald might now be a potential Cabinet minister of the 1990s, instead of a senior television executive flogging Take the High Road to an unsuspecting universe. Wasn't he sorry that he had chosen the media rather than politics?

"From my first days in journalism, I never regretted the choice. I was brought up agnostic and sceptical. I've never liked following crowds. I was trained to be independently minded. I wouldn't have been happy with the party faithful."

"So why did you work for Tribune?"

"You see, I worked for Tribune in my teens. And Tribune is very much..." Mr MacDonald paused. "I mean, don't forget that Michael Foot is the biographer of Swift and the lover of Hazlitt. And if you look at the cultural forces which shaped somebody like Nye Bevan, then you're into a non-conformist tradition which goes back a couple of centuries. I'm much closer to that tradition."

The more we talked about his political beliefs, the more ambivalent his answers became. I decided finally to put them to a simple, practical test. How did he feel about the future of Scotland? Would he welcome a parliament in Edinburgh?

"My scepticism," he replied, "has worked very well in journalism, and has given me the pleasant job of asking the questions all those years. So I don't hold strong opinions about which way Scotland should go, I don't hold strong opinions about most matters in public affairs. I keep an open mind, and I try to be an honest broker in presenting the information. I mean, I can see both sides of almost every question. That can be quite demobilising at times, but I don't regret it. In fact I rather enjoy the burden of being released from strong views about everything."

On the coffee table in Mr MacDonald's office, a number of papers and magazines were displayed. I glanced at them on the way out — but I couldn't see Tribune anywhere.

The Union Man

CAMPBELL CHRISTIE

Woodlands Terrace, Glasgow, is a street of fine offices and dark-suited men called consultants. I have never been sure what consultants are or do, but this area of the city — after Sauchiehall Street has run out but before the BBC and the University have begun — is full of them. Judging by the post-lunch street scene, everyone here is called Alastair and carries a vodophone.

Well, not quite everyone. At No. 16, in the heart of this executive ghetto, I found the headquarters of the Scottish Trades Union Congress. Inside, the dark, heavy wood seems to breathe half-forgotten glories. Beautifully woven union banners decorate the walls. It is a place of great, if melancholy, dignity.

"A grand building."

"Yes," said the General Secretary of the STUC, "but sometimes not very practical."

I followed him up a wide staircase into an enormous room dominated by a long table. This is where the leaders of Scottish trade unionism meet to discuss whatever is left for them to discuss after 10 years of Mrs Thatcher. In a corner, Campbell Christie has a desk facing the empty conference chamber. Notwithstanding his friendly, chubby presence, the ambience is decidedly gloomy.

Mr Christie returned to Scotland in 1986 as successor to the late Jimmy Milne. He had been in London for 15 years as a national officer of the Society of Civil and Public Servants.

"Did you want to come back very much?"

"I hadn't thought there was much likelihood of it. But when the opportunity arose, it didn't take me long to decide."

"And what did you think of Scotland? How had the place changed in those years?"

"Oh, fantastically. The whole structure of industry had changed. I left just before the UCS work-in. The de-industrialisation of the country hadn't started. We still had a coal-mining industry, a shipbuilding industry."

"You maintained an interest in Scotland while you were away?"

"Yes, but the thing was — it's useful to remember this — I didn't really know what was happening in Scotland. I had only a vague notion of how insecure and assembly-linked the newer industries were, only a broad idea of the political scene. That has influenced my thinking on the question of a Scottish parliament."

"How?"

"I really believe that most people in the south, including people at Westminster, haven't a clue what's going on up here. Even interested Scots in London don't know the detail. We need our own vision of what we are about."

Impressed by the prevailing ignorance — his own as well as others' — he became one of the keenest champions of devolution.

"Do you think the Labour Party really means it?"

"Yes."

"So if Mr Kinnock got into power in 1991 or 1992, he would set up a Scottish Assembly, would he?"

"He would."

"Mr Kinnock's never struck me as an enthusiast for the idea."

Mr Christie answered the question, adding with a laugh that what he had just said was not for quoting.

"Why not?"

"Well, I'll get into trouble for saying it!" I was not sure whether he was altogether serious. "But undoubtedly we would get a Scottish parliament if Labour were returned."

"Tam (Dalyell) might start being awkward about things."

"The West Lothian Question again."

"Exactly."

"Such is the movement in Scotland, no Labour MP in Scotland could afford to adopt the Dalyell line of the Seventies. He wouldn't get re-selected."

"The mood is that strong within the Labour Party?"

"Oh, yes. The mood for constitutional change is so strong that no

MP could stand against it."

Well, well. I had never heard it expressed quite like that before.

If Labour does somehow win the next election, Campbell Christie with his determination and clout will become one of the main architects of Scottish home-rule. He will carry more weight then than half a dozen Sillars. Yet he remains a comparatively unknown figure. Who is he, this man with the vision?

He was born in rural poverty, in a roadside cottage between Gatehouse-of-Fleet and Newton Stewart. The most beautiful drive in Scotland, Queen Victoria called it. A fine place to live, said Campbell Christie, if you had loads of loot.

"The cottage is still there?"

"It's now a country cottage for the local landowner."

His father blasted granite in an open quarry. If the weather was good and he worked, he was paid. If it rained, or he fell ill, he wasn't. He died at 42.

"What was the effect of his death on the family?"

"My mother was left with six boys to bring up. There was no sanitation, no water, no electricity. We had the big range, and oil lamps, an outside privy. We carried water from a well. We made life possible by working on the farms. My mother was a strong individual — though not in a physical sense."

"She had strength of character?"

"And a determination that her children shouldn't suffer the deprivations that she had. I remember her working on top of a threshing mill. We used to hoe turnips. And we would bunch snowdrops, and send them to Covent Garden market. You know the Cally Palace Hotel in Gatehouse? It was almost deserted during the war. We went there to pick snowdrops. One year we took some bulbs too, and re-planted them in the wood near the cottage so that they were easier to get at the next year. My mother would do whatever she could to make ends meet."

"Was it a political upbringing?"

"There was no strong political consciousness in the family. My father was a shop steward at the quarry, but he was really just one of the lads. So I didn't sit at anyone's knee while a great political debate went on, I didn't attend political meetings. But I did come to feel that society should treat people in a better way. I could identify with people at the bottom of the heap."

He started work as a civil servant with the Admiralty. Then came national service. Afterwards, he asked to join a department which would bring him into closer touch with people. They took him at his word, and sent him to the National Assistance Board. He became a visiting official: one of the breed known as the meany men.

"That was really what sparked my development politically. Just running hard up against poverty in Glasgow."

"You couldn't have been a terribly popular figure on the doorstep."

"In the main, I actually got on quite well. But there was a great frustration about the job. The official who was seen to be efficient in his work was the one who simply provided the minimum amount that people were entitled to. But the thing about National Assistance was the tremendous discretion allowed if you wanted to discover what people's exceptional needs were, and if you had the time." Such were the pressures of the work, staff rarely had the time.

"Do you think the divisions in society are as sharp now as they were then? Aren't most trade unionists pretty well off?"

"I'm not saying all workers are seriously exploited. But even among the employed, there are still divisions. Males in full-time employment are doing not too badly, but women, people working part-time, the peripheral workforce — they aren't doing well at all."

"How much has trade unionism changed since you became a full-time official? As disastrously as it seems?"

"Dramatically, in the sense that the trade union movement in the Fifties and Sixties, maybe even for part of the Seventies, was part of the consensus, much more part of the structure of society. Since that consensus broke down, our role has been more campaigning. Almost back to the original role of the trade union movement — to seek social justice and social change."

I wondered about that, in the summer of tube strikes in London, disruption on the railways, disaffected dockers and NALGO closing the Town Hall doors. I couldn't remember any one of these strikes being called to defend the Health Service.

"One of the problems," Mr Christie said, "is that we haven't adapted quickly enough to change."

He is not a naturally fluent speaker. His delivery can be laboured and repetitious. But on one subject at least, the General Secretary of the STUC is clarity itself. He has a definite view of the Scottish malaise and how to cure it.

"Absolutely," he agreed, when I challenged him on our lack of industrial creativity. "But in some part, that is the absence of a vision."

We were back to that.

"You think our branch-factory economy could be transformed by a Scottish parliament?"

"I think a Scottish parliament would give us the necessary focus. We lack coherence, in the sense of a structural arrangement that gives us the ability to work out policies."

"What about the SDA, or whatever it's called nowadays?"

"They're buffeted around from political crisis to political crisis."

"The regions?"

"The development of big regions like Strathclyde is perhaps helpful. But it's not an adequate substitute. What do we want in Scotland? We need a strategy."

"Tell me more about this parliament. Would you resurrect the Scotland Act of 1979 with all its well-known deficiencies?"

"No, no, no."

"What then?"

"The 1979 legislation gave Westminster a veto. What we want is a Scottish parliament that will have, not just devolved powers, but powers that once devolved are for the Scottish parliament to execute for good or ill."

"What sort of powers?"

"Economic powers. Powers to intervene — in other words, all the powers of the Industry Department for Scotland and the Department of Trade and Industry. Powers over grants and inducements to industry, powers over training. Even powers to raise money if that was thought appropriate..."

"It would collect taxes?"

"I'm not clear how you would link into UK taxation. There's a school of thought which says that we should collect all taxes in

Scotland and then pay Westminster for defence etc. rather than negotiate a block grant. Either way, we must have money that is managed in Scotland so that we determine our own priorities."

"You're coming pretty close to independence, aren't you?"

Mr Christie replied that independence as a first step was too dangerous a gamble and, he thought, unnecessary. Why not have common defence and foreign policies, a unified pensions and social security structure? The important thing was to manage our own affairs to the maximum extent that made sense.

"But you don't rule out independence at some future stage?"

"If it's clear, as a result of experience, that there's no reason why we shouldn't be independent, I'm prepared to enter into the debate. I don't say 'No'. I don't say 'Never'. Let's see first whether we can have a proper relationship with the other countries of the United Kingdom."

"How would you elect this parliament?"

"By proportional representation," he said eagerly.

"You're a fan of PR?"

"I wouldn't say I'm a fan, but I believe we want to unleash in Scotland forces of enthusiasm and drive and energy which would be lost if what we had was the old situation of one party saying, 'We've got the majority, we'll have our little group meeting, and then we'll do exactly what we want.'"

"That's pretty broad-minded considering Labour's natural majority in Scotland."

He was unrepentant about that. "The Labour Party's majority might be put at risk, but not a Left consensus. There is a broad consensus in Scotland that would want to do radical things. Of course, the worry about PR in some situations is that it gives tremendous power to a small minority. That's a legitimate argument. I admit it's a possible weakness. But in this case, I think the need to work with other forces would be a strength, not a weakness."

"What makes you think that?"

"Because we want to unify Scotland. We want to bring the Highlands and Islands into the picture, and the Borders, and Dumfries and Galloway. We want to create a cultural identity in Scotland. I think we could have a great driving force — a co-operative force that doesn't exist within the adversarial politics of Westminster."

After an hour with Mr Christie, his enthusiasm had become infectious. But as I left him to his vision, and walked into the late afternoon cool of Woodlands Terrace, I couldn't help thinking what the businesslike chaps with the vodophones would make of it all if it came to the crunch; to say nothing, of course, of the Leader of the Labour Party.

Smarter than the Average Bear

DAVID MURRAY

Under a burning sun, I went hunting for a surviving member of that rare and endangered species, the native entrepreneur. My expedition took me through a jungle of Japanese and American branch factories to the outskirts of Edinburgh, and an oasis of Scottish enterprise known as the South Gyle office park.

I finally tracked down the native entrepreneur to his administrative headquarters: a modern redbrick building with the names of 24 companies (all his) posted in the entrance hall. Inside, the atmosphere was almost unnervingly restful. A pretty girl, surrounded by greenery, sat answering the telephone. Behind her rose two semi-circular galleries in the style of a small opera house. But I found no prima donnas lurking behind the doors of the executive corridor; only purring computers and salad tables set for lunch.

The receptionist telephoned someone she called David to announce my arrival. David turned out to be no less than the native entrepreneur himself. A handsome, pugnacious Ayrshireman straight out of the pages of Burns, he wore a blue-striped shirt with the top button undone, no jacket, and a carelessly arranged red tie. He sat in a featureless office behind a big, tidy desk with a blotter covered in squiggles and figures.

Hot and tired, I began by asking a short, boring question ("What does Murray International Holdings consist of?") and sank back in my chair to await a long, boring reply. Instead, David Murray rattled off at top speed a telegramatic summary of his activities:

"Five main groups. Steel distribution. Metal testing. Office equipment. Property development. Manufacturing. Twelve hundred people. £100 million turnover. Profit of £6 million a year. Privately owned. Unusual in Scotland. I own 92 per cent, the other 8 per cent is owned by five Scottish institutions. That's the broad basis. I'll give you a video to take away for half an hour of back-up."

Disarmed by this spray of machine-gun fire, I could not bring myself to tell him that I did not possess a video player.

Still in his thirties, David Murray has already suffered two great traumas in his life. The first occurred at the age of 15, when he was prematurely uprooted from Fettes College.

"Regretfully, my father had hit bad times."

"How bad?"

"He'd been in business on his own. A coal merchant's in Ayr. He got involved in horse-racing. Through his own fault, he went bankrupt. Kaput."

"What happened to you then?"

"My mother and father split up and I finished my education at Broughton Secondary in Edinburgh. What helped me to survive was that I was quite good at sport. I was accepted more readily. You find out what you're made of, don't you?"

"How did you get on at Fettes?"

"I was about the only Scotsman there. They used to call me Jock. I was sport daft. Education-wise, mediocre."

"What can a private education supply that a state education can't?"

"Fine tuning. The extras. The teachers are no different, but the state school finishes at half past three, whereas my eldest boy, who's at Merchiston, is getting the benefit of being educated some nights till half past eight."

Academically undistinguished and deprived of his full course of fine tuning, Mr Murray began his working life as a trainee in a small metal business. When the owner sold the firm, the trainee decided to strike out on his own. "It was basically aluminium, then I moved into steel, buying ahead. In 1975, we turned over £2 million and made £100,000 net. A lot of money in those days. A lot of money today."

The startling facts of his youthful success were delivered in a fast tabloid style. He talked like a man who had formed a clear view of journalists' basic requirements. So when he described himself as a trainee in the small metal business, he was not simply a trainee, but, more helpfully, a "£7-a-week trainee".

"You make it all sound terribly easy."

"It was probably hellish at the time. Seems quite glamorous now."

"Didn't you ever worry that you'd go bust?"

"Near the edge a few times, but I've always had good bankers. I've had the Bank of Scotland with me since I was 22. The old adage is, if you've got a £, they'll lend you 50p. Every £ I had, the bank lent me £3."

He had been in business for less than a year when the second great trauma occurred. Returning from a rugby match in Dalkeith, he was bombing along the dual carriageway to Edinburgh when a tyre on his car exploded. (The front left tyre of a fibre-glass Lotus Elite, he volunteered with his usual attention to journalistic detail.) As the car collided with a tree at 80 m.p.h., he was thrown through the door.

"The guy I played rugby with was the anaesthetist, and my best man's wife was the nurse who took me in off the ambulance. They amputated through the knees that night. Then three days later, because there were a lot of twigs and stuff in the bone, they took me off above the knee. But there's plenty of people in the graveyard who'd swop places. I'm quite philosophical about it."

"But at the time?"

"I was so drugged I didn't know what philosophical meant. The funny thing was, I was getting taken back to the ward at half past one in the morning — they'd put 13 pints of blood into me — when I sat up in the wheelchair, not knowing my legs were off, and 'phoned my wife from a public 'phone box. Can you imagine that?"

"Tell me about your wife."

"She's been a big support. Met her at a party when she was 16 and I was 17."

"Is she involved in the business?"

"She keeps the home. I don't ever discuss business at home, and I never do business at home. Never have. Never, in all those years."

"How did you cope after the accident?"

"You just get on with it. You don't think about it."

"It had no effect on your life?" I asked disbelievingly.

"Well, I couldn't fail then, could I?" The imperturbable Mr Murray made the loss of both legs at the age of 23 sound like a business incentive scheme.

"You mean you consoled yourself that the worst had happened?"

"It couldn't get much worse, could it? Well, it could, but you don't think about that."

"Are you a religious man?"

"Not really. My faith was in my own ability."

I pressed him on the question of personal wealth. Was the accumulation of money important to him? Not at all important, he insisted. But had it been important to him when he didn't have any? No. If you started a business to make money, you wouldn't make any. The money should make itself.

He says he is an accumulator rather than a spender. He eats out fairly often and collects wine as a hobby, but invests most of his spare cash in property. I suggested to him he had been deeply influenced by what happened to his father.

"That was always a big factor," he agreed. "Definitely. He was a drinker. I don't drink excessively. I don't smoke cigarettes. I'm very cautious. The canny Scot, I'd like to think."

"A mean Scot?"

"Not a mean Scot!" (Laugh.)

"Is working hard important to you?"

"It's a way of life for me. I mean, every day I come in the door here, I'm pleased. Privileged. A lot of people are doing nothing every day, aren't they?"

"But what's the point of all this work?"

"Pride," he said with unexpected passion, departing for the first time from his staccato answers. "Pride in what I'm doing, pride in what I've built up. It's a Scottish success story. It's not about how much I'm worth, and all the rubbish that's written in the papers. It's a Scotsman that's doing this, and doing it in Scotland. We've had too many border raiders coming in, stealing our businesses. That's not happening at Murray International. Fifteen years ago, I employed one person. Today, I've got 1,200 and by the end of next year, it'll be 2,000. That's good. There's not enough of that."

As I listened to this outburst, all the more impressive for being genuinely felt, I found myself wondering whether Scotland really wants or even trusts people like David Murray. How come so much energy has been devoted to wooing foreign investment and so little to encouraging locally inspired enterprise? Does our national insecurity run so deep that in some twisted, unfathomable way we are actually happier as a branch factory economy?

I put these gloomy speculations to Mr Murray. He agreed that in Scotland success was resented, and found that as puzzling as I did. He thought our whole culture was wrong, that it tended to put too much emphasis on professional qualifications, teaching children how to become lawyers or accountants. There was no tradition of breeding entrepreneurs. Where were the new David Murrays in their twenties? Did I know of any? I said I didn't. If there were any, he said, they could start with him on Monday.

"What have you learned about managing people?"

"Never forget where you come from. Always give your top people part of the action. Pay peanuts and you get monkeys. Never bite the hand that feeds you. Lead by example. Always try and put yourself in their position. Bit corny, but true."

It appears to have worked for David Murray. Of the 25 senior executives who were with him 12 years ago, only three have left.

"Do you think the Scots are naturally hard working?"

"No, but the young are hungry. People generally expect handouts. We want money to be given to us."

"What about the poor?"

"I know there's a lot of poor people, and they need support. But nobody gave me a handout when I started."

"Are you a supporter of Mrs Thatcher?"

"I sometimes think she hasn't got the common touch, she doesn't really understand ordinary people's aspirations. But what's been the alternative? The majority have come a long way in 10 years. She's been the right person at the right time."

"Why do the Scots dislike her so much?"

"I don't think the message has got through."

★ ★ ★

A year ago, the native entrepreneur decided to do something for his native town. He offered to buy Ayr United Football Club, and convert the clapped-out little team in its clapped-out little stadium into something splendid and modern. He promised to spend a great deal of money to achieve this object. He vowed to put Ayr on the map. It seemed a fine, brave idea. There was only one problem: the board of Ayr United Football Club did not want Mr Murray or his grand plan. They were quite happy as they were, thank you very much.

"Did that hurt?"

"No. Because at the end of the day I've been proved right. The truth was that Ayr United were going nowhere."

"So you bought Rangers Football Club instead. That was bouncing back with a vengeance, wasn't it?"

"Graeme Souness, the manager, alerted me to the opportunity. If you're going to buy, buy the best, and Rangers is the best. It's a wonderful opportunity."

"Business opportunity?"

"Business and sporting. Rangers is a major brand name that has not been capitalised on. Yet."

"What do you think of the club's reputation as an enclave of Protestant Toryism?"

"That was maybe true in the past. Bigotry is a journalist's question."

"How?"

"People only want to criticise. We're going to change, but it'll take time. I'm not really interested in the politics and the history and the bigotry. What interests me is making Rangers the greatest football club in Europe. As long as the fans are true supporters of Rangers in football terms, that's all that really matters at the end of the day."

"Is it? I mean, football's not everything, is it?"

"To some people it is. What I like to think is that in 1981 when Rangers played Morton there were 5,000 people watching them. Now there's 45,000. The 40,000 who've come back aren't all bigots. It's just the minority spoiling it for the majority."

"What is the club's present policy about signing Catholic players?"

"If the player's good enough, we'll sign him. But we're not into tokenism. We will do it for the right reasons for Rangers Football

Club."

I had heard this answer so many times from successive Rangers managements that it was difficult to suppress a sour laugh. But when the interview was over, and the tape-recorder packed away, Mr Murray said enough to convince me of his good intentions. (A few weeks later, he proved them when Rangers signed the former Celtic player Mo Johnston, a Roman Catholic.)

"What do you think it takes to be a successful businessman?"

The native entrepreneur delivered his final telegram of the morning:

"Honest endeavour. A bit of flair. Being able to see the future. Hindsight — we've all got degrees in that. It's the clever man who can see ahead. I'm seeing opportunities ahead. Property trends. Business trends. Steel trends. Electronic trends. When you look at the video, you'll see that. I think that's where I've been a bit smarter than the average bear."

And with that he rose stiffly, fetched his crutches, and handed me the video.

Batons and Bludgeons

LORD HOME OF THE HIRSEL

The televising of the House of Lords, which has enabled the population at large to observe the British peerage in various stages of somnolence, has not affected the popularity of the institution. The upper chamber in its present form may be hard to defend in the name of democracy, but it is still a London tourist attraction of some magnetism. On the day of my appointment with one of its most revered members, there were two queues outside the Palace of Westminster. The queue awaiting admission to the House of Commons was the shorter.

"Obstinately," wrote Lord Home of the Hirsel, "the public seems to like a Lord." And no Lord is more liked than Lord Home himself — the perfect gent of British politics.

Now that there is an army of people called Bernard Ingham standing between the government and the media, it may not be possible any longer for a journalist to telephone a senior Cabinet minister and request his presence in a television studio. As recently as the early Seventies, however, matters were arranged more informally. One Sunday afternoon, an Icelandic cod war turned nasty, and my masters at BBC News ordered an interview with the Foreign Secretary. With some trepidation I telephoned Sir Alec (as he then was) at his home in the Borders and asked him if he would mind dropping everything to come to the Edinburgh studio. He was the soul of charm. He wouldn't mind at all. He was, he assured me, only doing the garden.

In the summer heat of London 15 years later, Lord Home,

elegantly pin-striped, was his usual courteous self. Would I like a cup of tea, perhaps? He was walking stiffly, but appeared otherwise extraordinarily fit for someone a few days short of his 86th birthday. He spends the early summer in London, though he told me that he didn't really know why, since there was nothing much to do.

"We'll go in here until we're thrown out," said the former Prime Minister, opening the door of a tiny room just off the Lords' main corridor.

"You once defined Conservatism as 'doing the right thing at the right time'. That doesn't strike a terribly ideological note, does it? Sounds rather pragmatic."

"I hope it sounds pragmatic. I meant it to be."

"Mrs Thatcher's not a pragmatist."

Lord Home paused. "I would have thought that she was. She's got her feet pretty firmly on the ground. But if I talked deeply, I wouldn't give that necessarily as my main feeling about Conservatism. I am, I hope, a realist and I think doing the right thing at the right time — what I call having a political nose — is a large part of politics. But not the whole."

"You also said once that politics is a profession not for the bully with a bludgeon, but for the artist with a baton. Doesn't Mrs Thatcher have a tendency to bludgeon?"

"She's very blunt, and straightforward," he said, ever the diplomat. "There are times when this is very valuable. There are times, too, when somebody with the political arts of Harold Macmillan comes in. So I wouldn't say that one's exclusive of the other. I think you want to be direct at times and give very definite leadership. I doubt if a man would have carried through the Falklands campaign."

"Really?"

"Well, it wanted a woman to disregard all the terrible hazards that would have been obvious to any man. But she did it, and all credit to her. She is a very striking and forthright politician."

"Macmillan was a healer though, wasn't he? He felt strongly about unemployment. He wanted to heal the divisions in society."

"Hmmm."

"And you were, too. But Mrs Thatcher doesn't seem to be a healer in that old, humane Conservative tradition."

"I think whatever impression she gives, she is actually. She's a very humane woman, and a very nice woman. And curiously enough, under the humane dispensation, we had neglected some pretty dangerous elements in our society. Or at any rate, hadn't dealt with them."

"Such as?"

"Such as the..." He tapped his fingers on the tape recorder, searching for the word. "...the young...the permissive society. That had run along without any discipline. And the difficulties over the trade unions. We tried hard — Mrs Castle tried hard, too — to get rules which would enable them to play a reasonable part in our society. But we ignored their massive power, and their abuse of power, for too long. Mrs Thatcher seized on that, and dealt with it."

Not from Lord Home the disloyalty of a Heath. But when I asked him to name the Prime Minister he had most admired in his political career, it was not Mrs Thatcher he chose, but a man who preferred the baton to the bludgeon.

"In the domestic field, Mr Baldwin," he replied unhesitatingly. "I thought he was an artist at domestic politics. In particular, I saw him deal with the General Strike of 1926. Immaculate, his handling of that. The opposition at that time was led by Mr Lansbury. The weakest opposition, perhaps, that we'd ever had. Mr Baldwin treated them with kid gloves, brought them round, and enabled the socialists to remain constitutional. A very artistic performance."

"But not so effective internationally?"

"Oh, he didn't like foreigners. Didn't really care for international affairs, therefore neglected them. That was very damaging on the road up to the 1939 war. The historians are almost certain to say that Baldwin's government ought to have started re-armament two or three years earlier. I don't think, as a matter of fact, that it would have prevented war, but it would have given us a better chance to be prepared than we were in 1938, when it was almost too late to do anything."

Lord Home has been around for as long as most of the momentous events of the 20th century, and a participant in several of them. As a young MP, he accompanied Chamberlain to Munich for the last fateful meeting with Hitler. He remembers the peculiar way in which Hitler walked — his arms hung low, almost to his knees, and swinging not alternately but in unison — and how animal it made him look.

"Chamberlain's attempt at what is now called appeasement was mainly designed to persuade Hitler that if he contemplated making war, Germany would be the country which would suffer, and that central Europe would be wide open to Communist penetration. Chamberlain thought that this must influence Hitler's thinking. Of course, he was wrong, and you're not forgiven by the public if you're wrong."

"What did the experience teach you?"

"That No. 10 and the Foreign Office should keep in the closest possible touch, so that they do not diverge in their interpretation of what action should be taken in foreign affairs. When it came to the time when I was Foreign Secretary and Harold Macmillan was Prime Minister, I always used to insist on going to drink a glass of sherry with him once a week, outside Cabinet hours, to make absolutely sure that we were pursuing the same lines of policy."

"Do Prime Ministers interfere too much in foreign policy?"

"There's no use complaining about it. They have since a long way back. A number of Prime Ministers do their acting in foreign fields."

Lord Home was Foreign Secretary in two post-war Conservative governments (Heath's as well as Macmillan's) and one of the leading players in arms negotiations with the Russians. In his memoirs, published in 1976, his mistrust of Russian motives, and disillusionment over the painfully limited progress of talks to end the Cold War, were obvious on page after page:

"Russia's Empire is occupied by military force and ruled by fear"/"Russia's colonialism is the most cruel and ruthless in history"/"It is difficult not to despair when faced with such a record of duplicity by the Communists"/"When a Russian does not wish to act he will use any device to stall"/"The Russians had cheated for the third time"/"Let up for one moment on vigilance, and everything which we value could be lost in the twinkling of an eye". And much, much else in the same hawkish vein. I asked Lord Home whether the actions of the present Soviet leadership had caused him to soften his views.

"Mr Gorbachev is different from any of the Russian hierarchy that I've met before, in that he will argue. Old Gromyko and co., whenever I used to say that Communism wanted a lot more explanation than they'd given me, now what about it, would always reply that it was not appropriate to speak on subjects of that kind, and that was that. Down came the Iron Curtain. But this man will laugh, and try and justify the Communist experiment. He's a much more flexible character. Whether he is a Communist in the sense that the others were, I am not sure."

"You thought at one time that it was the Communists' business to undermine. Do you still think that?"

"I think that the aim of the Soviet Union, realistically now, cannot be to undermine the stability of the world. I think they've had to admit defeat on that."

This was a rather bleak acknowledgement of the change in the Soviet will. And when I went on to seek Lord Home's assessment of the prospects for peace between East and West, his optimism was heavily qualified.

"There's a better prospect," he said cautiously. "How real it's going to turn out to be, I don't know. In terms of disarmament — which is one way of measuring the progress made — probably Mr Gorbachev is genuinely interested. But an awful lot will depend on how far he is willing to try and arrive at an equality between East and West on the conventional weapons front. That's what all the trouble's been about, this mass of stuff mobilised on the eastern frontier of West Germany. If he can bring himself to try and get a genuine, mutual and balanced disarmament — the formula Gromyko always refused to recognise when I used to talk to him about it — that will make a difference."

"What is Britain's influence in the modern world? Shorn of most of our political and economic muscle, what role is there left for us to play?"

"As a partner in Europe and as a particular friend of the United States. And of course, although the Commonwealth is an intangible collection of countries, nevertheless it is a good thing to be a member of that organisation, which is global after all, and embraces countries with many forms of government. It does give a certain prestige to this country to be the recognised leader of the Commonwealth."

"You mentioned Europe first. But the present Conservative leadership is pretty hostile to Europe. Does that bother you?"

"We're legislating in this matter for a hundred years, more

perhaps, and therefore we must make sure that at every step we get it right. The enthusiasts always want to set time-tables to achieve certain objectives. I don't think that is the best way to go about it. I think we go slowly, consolidating every step behind us as we take it."

"How far would you go towards European political union?"

"It shouldn't be federalist. I was introduced to Europe by de Gaulle. He was always anti-federalist. He thought you must retain patriotism which identified the citizen of the country in which he lived. I agree."

"No United States of Europe, ever?"

"No. I think our history militates against that. But we can do an awful lot on the economic side, and a certain amount on the political."

It was only in his old age that Lord Home began to enjoy rave reviews. At the height of his political career, he had to endure the sort of press ridicule and contempt reserved these days for the extreme left-wing. When Macmillan appointed him Foreign Secretary in 1960 (he was a hereditary peer at the time), one journalist wrote: 'Never since Caligula appointed his horse a consul has a political office been so abused.' Then the impossible happened. In 1963, the year that sex was invented (so Philip Larkin said), ladies of easy virtue could still endanger the stability of the state, and a 14th Earl could still become Prime Minister.

Also that year, That Was the Week That Was launched the age of satire; and the new Prime Minister was an irresistible target.

He found that he was not telegenic. One conversation with a BBC make-up girl went like this:

Q: Can you not make me look better than I do on television?

A: No.

Q: Why not?

A: Because you have a head like a skull.

Q. Does not everyone have a head like a skull?

A. No.

Not only did he have a head like a skull; he also wore half-moon spectacles. His wife Elizabeth always insisted that those spectacles lost him the 1964 general election.

"Do you think you were a victim of your television image? That perhaps you were the first victim of television politics?"

"I never dreamt I was going to be Prime Minister, so I never took all that much trouble about the media. Obviously I was wrong. But I was never attracted by television. I always thought it was very superficial. They give you about two minutes to talk about world problems! But though I don't like it, I think you can turn it to good effect. President Reagan and Harold Wilson to some extent learned how to use the thing."

"Do you like it any more now?"

"Still don't care for it. I don't like politics conducted or much influenced by the media."

"How has it affected politics?"

"Not much, in the sense that the programme of any governing party is conducted still through the Cabinet and through Parliament, and all that. But the relationship between the politician and the public, which is an important part of politics, has certainly been affected, and I would guess adversely. I've often wondered how Winston would have dealt with television."

"How would he, do you imagine?"

"I think he'd have kicked the machine, probably!"

"Do you feel that you didn't get a chance as Prime Minister?"

"Well, I'd like to have had longer to do a few things," said Lord Home with his customary good humour, "but the trouble was there was nothing to do that year. We'd finished our legislative programme, and you couldn't start a new programme in under a year. It was just one of those things in politics."

He fought a good campaign in 1964, only just losing to Harold Wilson. And he won one notable war of words. When Mr Wilson taunted him with being the 14th Earl, Sir Alec retorted that doubtless his opponent was the 14th Mr Wilson.

If only he had listened to his father, and contented himself with running the family's great Border estate, he would have spared himself such unpleasantness.

"My father was as near a saint as you could find. His advice to me was: 'Before you act, always ask yourself what effect your action's going to have on the other fellow.' That's an interpretation of Christian values. He thought politics was a dirty business."

"But you didn't agree with him?"

"I saw this as a very unfair argument. Even if it was a dirty business, why not go in and clean it up!"

Lord Home has been attempting to clean it up for the last 58 years, ever since his first election as MP for Lanark. So far, however, the body politic has not responded kindly. It has remained more or less its usual grubby self.

"Is the standard of Parliamentary debating as good as it was when you entered politics?"

"The debates I heard in the Thirties were of a higher standard — a good deal higher. Partly because 90% of the business now is about economics. It's not easy to make great oratorical speeches about economics. Not easy to be inspired."

"Who do you remember from that era?"

"The first person I heard in the House of Commons when I walked in in 1931 was Hugh Cecil, one of the old-style orators. Baldwin I remember sitting on the front bench alone. Very empty house. And Hugh got up — it was some Bill, can't remember what — and said, 'If the Right Honourable Gentleman persists in this ridiculous Bill which he wishes to make an Act of Parliament, there will be only one prospect for England — to look down upon a vista of humble pies!'. You could just see these things stretching into the distance!"

"Who was the best Parliamentary speaker you heard?"

"Well, Hugh Cecil was one. Maxton was another. A very effective Parliamentarian. There were the three Red Clydesiders: Maxton, Stephen and McGovern. High-class lot. Maxton and Stephen in particular. They were Glasgow University boys. They had finesse, they were very artistic. McGovern was rather a bludgeon man."

"You liked Maxton a lot?"

"I had quite a soft spot for him, yes."

"Were there any other socialists you liked?"

"Yes. Attlee. A man of decision and very few words. I remember Stafford Cripps telling me one day he'd been into Attlee's room on some business. He politely turned to the door and said, 'Anything more I can do for you, Prime Minister?' And the answer was, 'Yes, go.' Typical Attlee! But he was a very authoritative, thoughtful fellow, who did very well. And Winston thought highly of him, too, although he made endless jokes about him. But never mind: he relied on him a lot as Deputy Prime Minister during the war."

In 1968, the year after the Scottish nationalists' unexpected victory in the Hamilton by-election, Mr Heath, then Leader of the Opposition, asked Sir Alec to chair a Conservative Party committee on the future of Scotland's government. Later that year, at the Scottish Tory conference, Mr Heath made what he called "The Declaration of Perth", accepting the committee's recommendation for a directly elected Scottish Assembly, with legislative powers.

In his memoirs eight years later, Sir Alec thought the idea so important that he devoted a chapter to it, expressing his disappointment that nothing had been done. Given the present leadership's strongly expressed antipathy to devolution, I was curious to know whether the party's elder statesman still harbours home-rule sentiments.

"I've always been a decentraliser," he said, "and always hoped that we could devise some form of devolution which would meet the legitimate aspirations of the Scottish people. And of course, the creation of the Secretary of State's office and the Scottish Office was meant to supply this devolution. To my mind, if the Ministers of State are allowed to move around Scotland and explain policy, that ought really to be good enough."

The vision of Michael Forsyth as the great evangelist of the Scottish people seemed at first blush somewhat unlikely. But let that pass: for what was more interesting was Lord Home's complete volte-face on the subject.

His memoirs, which I had read on the train south, were still fresh in my mind.

"We rejected," he wrote, "an Assembly which would be purely consultative...we felt that moderate Scottish opinion would not be satisfied unless the Assembly had a part in shaping that legislation which applied specifically to Scottish affairs...Political devolution is unreal unless it involves some delegation of control over funds, and we strongly recommended that a block grant for Scotland should be provided..."

So what has changed?

"It's very difficult," he said. "The committee I chaired could only come out with this one proposal: that purely Scottish Bills, as defined by the Speaker, would be taken in their early stages in a Scottish Assembly, and then sent to Westminster to complete their Parliamentary passage. But we all thought it was clumsy, and recommended it without much confidence. It didn't catch on."

I was still puzzled. For there was no reference in the memoirs to a lack of confidence in the idea; no suggestion of clumsiness. Then I remembered what he had said earlier in our conversation about the importance of a political nose, and concluded that Lord Home's must be as sensitive as ever to the mood of his party.

"So what do you propose now?".

"I don't think that I could confidently recommend any development to improve on the Secretary of State and his Office."

"But you acknowledge that there is a substantial minority of Scots who wish to see an independent Scotland?"

"I always thought the Scots knew which way their bread was buttered. I thought that was their characteristic. No borderer would like to see frontiers resurrected — we suffered enough from the separation of the two countries. But if the Scots were really to be independent, I think it would be plumb crazy. I remember when Winston sent me up there. 'Go and quell those turbulent Scots,' he said, 'and don't come back till you've done it.'"

"They're still turbulent."

"Yes, but a lot of the secret is explanation. The present Secretary of State is the most articulate I've ever heard, I think — and I hope that things will settle down and be better. But I'm sure that separation is a nonsense."

And there we left it.

"Faith in God is important to you. Do you think that Britain is necessarily a poorer place for being an increasingly secular one?"

"Yes, I do, but a lot of young people are now understanding that life is incomplete unless they have faith in something beyond this life. So I don't despair at all."

"What about the state of Britain generally?"

"The enterprise of the young encourages me. What discourages me is that as a nation we are getting older and older, and fewer people are having to earn the wealth necessary to establish the standards we want."

"Aren't we in danger of forgetting about the poor?"

"That could be a danger, yes. But we are actually deploying more in terms of cash and hardware to the social services than we ever have before. I come back to the important thing: we've got to earn the wealth, however hard and material that may sound. That's why basically Mrs Thatcher is right."

At the end of our chat, Lord Home returned to the chamber to rejoin a debate on the privatisation of the electricity industry. He has outlived most of the historic figures of world politics he talked about during our hour together. Churchill, de Gaulle, Macmillan, Baldwin, Chamberlain, Attlee, Gromyko — all gone. On a political stage increasingly dominated by the bludgeon, he has become perhaps the last of the old artists.

Outside in the sun, the queue was as long as ever.

A lot of luck

HAMISH MacINNES

"Meeting you in Glencoe could be tricky," said Hamish MacInnes on the telephone. "There's no guarantee I'll be there when you arrive." After a puzzled silence at my end, he added helpfully: "If there's a rescue on..."

Ah, yes. Stupid of me. In the end, I met the leader of the Glencoe mountain rescue team in a lounge of the Central Hotel in Glasgow — not quite the evocative setting I had intended. The only people who looked as if they might have needed rescuing were a party of OAPs in search of an Age Concern meeting.

Six years short of being an OAP himself, Mr MacInnes is still admirably fit and lithe. He was in Glasgow to do a spot of post-production work for a film he is making for the BBC. He says he is fed up writing books, and intends to spend the next two years exploring and filming in lonely places. He has formed an independent production company for this purpose.

"Are you a solitary individual?"

"To some extent, I suppose I am. Some of my work — photography, for example — is essentially a lonely business."

"Do you like lonely places?"

"Probably my favourite place in the world is the upper Amazon. The rain forest is fascinating. Been in and out of it quite a few times."

"Tell me about your first visit."

"It was quite frightening. So many spiders, scorpions and snakes...an abundance of everything that creeps and crawls such as

I'd never found anywhere else. Unbelievable. I needed a lot of persuasion to go back."

"So why did you?"

"Because the exploration side is so interesting. Going to places no one's been before. It's very hard to make progress, and it's only climbers who can get down through those gorges."

"There can't be many places left where no one's been before."

"That's about the only place, actually. There are quite large tracts which are still unexplored. They are very, very inhospitable. Nobody could possibly live in them."

It is hard to say where Hamish MacInnes picked up his venturesome spirit. There appears to have been nothing in his background or upbringing to suggest that he would become one of Scotland's most celebrated explorers and climbers. His father was a small shopkeeper; he could have ended up doing nothing more exciting with his life than running the family stationers.

"I was born in Gatehouse-of-Fleet. My parents were from the Highlands — my mother from Skye, my father from Lochaber — so that's where my roots are. I don't really know why they settled in Gatehouse."

"Were they Gaelic speakers?"

"Yes. Especially when they were saying something I wasn't supposed to hear."

"Did you like your father?"

"I can't say I did. He was a slightly hard man, though very fair. He spent a long time in the trenches at Passchendaele during the first world war and saw virtually everybody around him die. After that, he became very religious. I rebelled, as children of religious fathers often do."

"How did you rebel?"

"Well, perhaps rebel is too strong a word. But when you have religion for breakfast, lunch and tea, there's a natural rejection of it. I rejected it."

At the age of 14, the family moved to Greenock. He found that claustrophobic, particularly as he was beginning to acquire an interest in the outdoors. An income tax inspector called Bill Hargreaves, who was also a fine mountaineer, taught him to climb. "Bill was a good tutor," he remembers. "He put some sense into me."

"How far did you have to travel?"

"The first climbing I did was on the Cobbler, then I went to Glencoe. That was quite energetic. I cycled from Greenock to Glencoe for the weekend, climbed all weekend, then cycled back again. Pretty strenuous if there was a head wind on the Rannoch Moor. Which there invariably was."

"What did you like about climbing?"

He said he found that difficult to explain. You either took to it or you didn't. He thought it might have something to do with the freedom it allowed.

"Were you escaping from something?"

"Perhaps. It's interesting that most of the best climbers are from cities."

His first big expedition was illegal. In 1953 he and John Cunningham, another notable Scottish climber, decided to make an attempt on Everest despite being refused permission by the Nepal government. "The rule was you weren't allowed in unless you had Himalayan experience, but of course you couldn't get experience unless you went to the Himalayas...an absolutely ridiculous set-up. But we'd heard that a previous, Swiss-led expedition had left a large cache of food on camp 2 and being Scots, we thought we'd go in search of the food." They trained hard in New Zealand for six weeks, then made their unauthorised entry into the Himalayas — only to discover that John Hunt's expedition had got there before them.

"The food was gone?"

"They'd used the lot. Bit of a disaster in that respect."

Twenty two years later, on another Everest climb, he almost died when he was caught in an avalanche 26,000 feet up. The rope held, otherwise he surely would have perished, but the after-effects of powder in the lungs badly damaged the cartilages of his rib cage. Another climber died in the expedition.

"This element of danger. Could it be part of the attraction?"

"Difficult situations certainly get the adrenalin flowing. In retrospect, maybe you find that satisfying — pushing yourself a bit beyond what you thought you were capable of."

"And yet you've seen many colleagues killed..."

"It's amazing. I was speaking to Chris Bonington about this just the other day. Between the two of us, we've lost over 30 close friends. In fact, of all the people I started climbing with seriously, Chris is the only one left. Everybody else is dead."

"Are you afraid of dying on a mountain?"

"Not in the least."

"Why not?"

"I don't know. Probably because I'm fairly close to it most of the time."

"Close to death?"

"Well, to fairly dangerous situations. In rescue work, for instance. But it never bothers me in the least. If you go, you go. That's it."

When he went to live in Glencoe in 1959, he found that mountain rescues were organised ad hoc, that the rescuers were poorly equipped, and that in the absence of telephones the alarm was raised by bicycle. Ernest Marples, Postmaster General of the day and a keen hill-walker, was prevailed upon to give Glencoe the telephone. Hamish MacInnes did most of the rest.

"We operate a radio call-out system. Very efficient. We each carry a small set with us — especially if we're on the mountains."

"How do you go about rescuing a climber?"

"Modern technology is important. Initially we relied on getting people down in a fairly antiquated way. The stretchers were too clumsy and heavy, so I made a folding, portable stretcher which is now used all over the world. That was a big step forward. Then the helicopters came. They're an essential feature of rescue work."

"Are weekend climbers still doing daft things on mountains?"

"Not so much. But the essence of winter climbing, especially at this latitude, is speed. People don't realise that the winter day is so short, and they tend to go over-equipped — they carry the most enormous rucksacks. That slows them down."

"But otherwise they're fairly responsible?"

"Well, one quality we're losing is dedication to one's companions. Quite frequently now, we rescue climbers who've been...well, not exactly abandoned by their friends. But let's say their friends didn't show great charity in helping them. That's very offputting."

"You mean people are just left up there?"

"I've come across cases where a member of a party has fallen, and the others haven't even looked for him. Particularly if the conditions are bad, they'll just come back to fetch help. This is one of the unfortunate things about sophisticated rescue work — people tend to leave it to the rescuers. Which is all very well, but there's a certain responsibility to one's companions. When I started climbing and something happened, we did our damndest to get the person down the mountain. We were brought up to help one another."

Even in the high mountains, it seems there is no escape from the selfishness of the human race.

A group of men in business suits had arrived at the next table. They were laughing so loudly that I had to strain to hear Hamish MacInnes describe in his soft voice the more hair-raising details of his hazardous existence. It was the hour of morning coffee, a far cry from the rain forest of the upper Amazon, and Mr MacInnes had an odd ability to express the realities of danger and death in a flat, almost detached conversational style. It did not feel like the time or the place to discuss the nature of heroism in the modern world. But I decided to raise the subject anyhow.

"Mountaineering at its best is regarded as a heroic activity. Do you agree?"

"Heroism is difficult to define. It's often something that happens in the heat of the moment, something one does instinctively. Look at it from the rescue point of view. Basically, the reason one goes rescuing is because one likes doing it. There's no real heroism in that."

"Seriously?"

"Well, yes. If we're involved in a difficult rescue it's reported in newspapers all over the country. The real heroes are people who look after spastics or the terminally ill, but get no thanks at all."

"What about achieving a summit? That's surely a symbol of great heroism, isn't it?"

"Heroism doesn't come into it. That's all about personal ambition, endurance, fitness."

"And luck?"

"I certainly agree with that."

"And you've had more than your fair share of it?"

"I've been involved in five avalanches. To survive one

avalanche, you have to be very lucky. Another thing — I've had all sorts of accidents. For example, a few years ago I had an impact injury on my legs which turned out to be gas gangrene. It was something like 50 hours before it was diagnosed. I shouldn't be alive today after that. But six months later, I was climbing Everest with a big aluminium plate over the wound. So, yes, a lot of luck. And when your time's up, it's up. There's no worrying about it."

"So you haven't discovered God on top of a mountain?"

"No, I'm an atheist. I'm interested in all sorts of religions, I even lived in a Himalayan monastery for a short period, but I've never followed any of them up. My father wasn't particularly religious until his war experience. Well, I've been close to death too, in a slightly different way of course, but it's had the opposite effect on me. I've gone to the other extreme."

"I wonder why?"

"Religion's a kind of weakness, perhaps. I feel I can set my own standard of values of how I want to conduct my life — and I don't need the crutch of religion to make me stay on that path. So I just haven't felt the need to believe in a God."

If I were Hamish MacInnes, I would be thinking that somebody up there must like me.

Thumping the table

VERY REV. THOMAS TORRANCE

"When did you first believe in God?"

"I always believed. I remember lying on the lawn of our house in China, looking up at heaven and thinking about God the creator of the universe. I think that was my earliest conscious memory."

"What age were you?"

"I must have been about six."

Seventy years later, the boy on the Chinese lawn has become the Very Reverend Thomas F. Torrance, theologian, former Moderator of the General Assembly of the Church of Scotland, Emeritus Professor of Christian Dogmatics at Edinburgh University, and owner of a rare and dazzling collection of doctorates. He is a Dr Theol, a DLitt, a DD, a DrTeol, a DTheol and a DSc.

I met him in the attic of his house in the Braids, as near heaven as suburban Edinburgh is likely to get. The Professor's two dogs barked a lusty greeting at the door and followed me all the way upstairs, licking me eagerly as I broached the vexed questions of God, death and the after life.

The attic, which enjoys a fine view over the city to the Forth bridges and Fife, is somewhat spartan in decor. Neatly arranged on shelves almost ceiling high are thousands of theological books and journals. That the floorboards have not collapsed under the weight of so much wisdom says much for the householder's faith.

In a far corner, opposite the antiquarian section, Professor Torrance sits at a word processor tapping out his books, articles and pamphlets. He is an enthusiast for computer technology, and told me much of interest about the economics and technicalities of desktop publishing and laser printing.

On a map of China above the word processor, he pointed out the old provincial city of Chengdu, where he was born and brought up, one of six children of Christian missionaries. His parents were immense influences in his life. He describes his father as an evangelist to the core, but considers his mother (an Anglican) the deeper theologian. When they argued about bishops, as they often did, it was his father who got the worst of it and retreated crestfallen to the garden, muttering to young Tom about his mother and her bishops.

"My father went out on January 1, 1896. He ran a mission in the Alpine mountains of West China, and that's where we lived. I didn't leave China until I was 14."

"What was it like?"

"We spent the winter in the plain. In the summer, we went into the mountains to get away from the heat and the disease. Up there, there were wild strawberries, and kiwi fruit, and more Alpine flora than you could find in any other part of the world. It was really a very lovely place."

"What about the natives?"

"Some of my memories are pretty shocking. There were civil wars going on all the time. I saw people having their heads whipped off with swords. Life was very cheap. Hands were cut off for theft. I used to ride on horseback to school three miles every day, and was always stumbling on little baby girls, dead in the grass."

"Were you in great danger?"

"Some of the Chinese mobs were quite unbelievable. I can still see them at our door, howling for blood. And father fending them off with words! We were driven out in 1927 when Chiang Kai-shek took over. Some of our missionaries were hung. There was a lot of martyrdom. Then my father went back for seven years on his own, while mother stayed at home to look after us. Just as he retired in 1935, there was the Long March, and they destroyed all the churches he had built, shot all the pastors."

Tom Torrance completed his schooling in Scotland, gradually coming to terms with the odder Scottish customs. In his first week, he upset his mother when he returned from a shopping errand empty-handed and explained that the shopkeeper had thrown him out. "Well I'd started to bargain with them. We always bargained in China!"

He decided that he would go to Tibet, and become a missionary.

"Do you think faith is a gift?"

"I think faith is quite natural. When you're brought up to it, as I was, it becomes very deeply instinctive. I have never had — people think this is crazy — I have never had any doubts."

"No crisis of faith at all? No difficulty?"

"Absolutely certain, always," he insisted, smiling serenely. Then he thumped the flat of his hand on the table beside him. "Just as certain as that table." It was a solid piece of furniture, and held steady against the theologian's blow. "You don't have doubts about your own existence or the realities around you. God's just like that."

"Do you pray a lot?"

"I have a sanctuary here. I find I need to pray on my knees, and I pray morning and night. I usually read at least five chapters of the Bible every day, reflect on them, and pray."

When I said I hadn't noticed the sanctuary, Professor Torrance rose and took me to it. It is in a dark, hidden place behind the books, on the other side of the attic from the word processor.

I said something banal about science and religion co-existing.

"Science and theology," he corrected me. How terrifying it must have been, it suddenly occurred to me, to have had this formidable intellectual as one's Professor of Christian Dogmatics.

"Do you find praying fairly peaceful?"

"On the whole, very. But there are occasions when prayer is an agony. Then you believe that you really are in touch with God, asking and receiving."

"So we're quite entitled to expect our prayers to be answered?"

"Well, they have to be prayers in accordance with the will of God, and the will of God doesn't only concern us as individuals."

With this enigmatic qualification, we returned to our afternoon tea at the table by the window, the table as solid and unshakeable as the Professor's faith. And I wondered aloud about Christians who could not share his enviable certainty, who openly expressed their doubts. What did a hard thump on the attic table do for them?

"Unfortunately," said Professor Torrance, brisk as an Edinburgh breeze, "the general framework of our culture is derived from old-fashioned Newtonian science, that anything you can't explain in hard causal terms, you can't accept. Of course I wasn't brought up to that, I didn't have that kind of cultural framework. But I can understand that many people are like that. I remember one of my own sons coming home from school one day and asking me, 'How do you prove God exists?' And I said 'Well, if you could prove it, it wouldn't be God you were talking about. You can't prove Him.' Years later, he said to me that he had no problems after that."

Though he never fulfilled his Tibetan ambition, Tom Torrance travelled widely and eventfully. In 1936, while visiting the Middle East as a student, he was arrested as a suspected Jewish spy and sentenced to death. Having got himself out of that, he celebrated freedom by stumbling unsuspectingly into a brothel. There were further adventures reminiscent of an Evelyn Waugh novel, before a brief and trouble-free idyll as a parish minister in Perthshire.

In 1943, he was off again — sailing from Liverpool as a Church of Scotland chaplain.

He recalled his wartime exploits in a quick succession of understatements. He "got stuck" in Algiers, "went over to Alexandria", "raced back to Tripoli", "stayed in Palestine for a bit", "finished up in Italy". Described with such sang froid, Tom Torrance's war could almost be mistaken for a jaunt. Jaunt it wasn't.

"Did you witness a lot of suffering?"

"Well, yes. Italy was particularly tough, because I was with the infantry units and usually went with them into action as a stretcher-bearer. Most of the fighting was at night, and very close. When wounded men were machine-gunned on the ground by the Germans, that was terrible. Really traumatic."

But the faith first glimpsed under a Chinese heaven never deserted him. He tended the wounded as best he could, applying a crude penicillin powder to huge, gaping wounds, then watched awe-struck as the flesh renewed itself. "This horrible, stinking mess...and yet somehow, incredibly, God was operating in it, re-creating the whole of our life and existence underneath." When he returned to Scotland, he preached on this powerful but daunting metaphor.

He never killed. Might he have killed?

"I had to make up my mind that if it came to the point, I would have had to be shot rather than shoot. That's my faith and my belief."

"You tended to the dying..."

"That was harrowing. I remember after one night engagement, I found a young man dying. He could only have been 18. He knew he was dying. He looked up at my face, and asked, 'Padre, is God really like Jesus?' And I replied, 'Yes.' And, in the few minutes we had left together, I spoke to him about it. After the war, an old, dying lady in Aberdeen asked me exactly the same question. So there it was — in civilian life, in the battlefield — the same basic issue, the deepest question of the human heart."

"How do you answer it?"

"By telling them that Jesus loves them and forgives them, that He is gracious and kind. But is there behind the back of Jesus, a God who is unknown, a terrifying deity? Unfortunately, that is the kind of God Calvinism has often worked with. There is no such God. There is no God behind the back of Jesus. There is only one God, the God shown in the face of Jesus. That has been absolutely central in my mission all the way through."

Perhaps, I suggested, what troubled the dying soldier and the old lady in Aberdeen was the amount of suffering created in the world by this gracious, kind and loving God. Professor Torrance said that was a question which came up all the time. He gave me a long and complex answer — something about evil being an unnatural break in lines of continuity — which eventually lost me. "I have no great difficulty helping educated people to understand these questions," he said finally, "but when you come down to people who are not accustomed to thinking in that way, that's more difficult." Now I knew I would never make a theologian. "At this point," he continued, "all we can do is to point them to the cross of Christ and say, 'We can't explain evil. God has never explained it. What we do know is that God has come into the midst of it and granted us salvation from it.' And, of course, this is true theologically."

But it still didn't seem to this untrained mind a totally satisfactory answer.

"Maybe the reason there's so much suffering in the world is

because God's not like Jesus. Maybe He's a Calvinist after all. A bit of a hard man."

"No. The opposite. Because the God of the cross refused to keep aloof from our agony, our hurt, our shame, our misery, our violence, but came into the midst of it, took it upon Himself. That's a God of utter compassion and unlimited love."

We left God and talked a bit about something quite different, the state of institutional Christianity. Professor Torrance sounded close to despair about that. He said with his customary power and conviction that there was no question about it, the Church was in terrible disarray. In trying to make the Gospel relevant to modern man, it had itself become increasingly secular. Some of the stuff being preached from the pulpits you could read in the Sunday newspapers. He added, with a grim chuckle, that teachers of divinity had a lot to answer for.

That took him naturally to his favourite theme, the attempt to reconcile science and theology. It was a staggering fact, he said, that today scientists were more and more the believers, churchmen less and less so. In America, where he had given a series of lectures, he had found that many in the congregation were scientists.

"At the end, one of them asked me, 'Dr Torrance, how do you regard yourself?' I said to him, 'Well, I'm just an evangelist.' 'What?' He sounded surprised. 'Well,' I said, 'my task nowadays is to evangelise theologians and scientists. But I will say that it's much more difficult to evangelise the theologians.' There was the greatest outburst of spontaneous laughter! They were the believers! But the Church can't cope with it."

"Do you think about death at all?"

"I never did, but at my age, you do begin to think about it. In a way you look forward to it. You get tired and weary and want a rest. And the joy of being in the new creation, the risen life, where we don't have all these problems..." Professor Torrance paused, and confessed with a small sigh that he was being selfish. We were sent here to cope with the problems...

My mind went back to the picture of the boy on the Chinese lawn, looking up at heaven.

"Can you tell me about heaven?"

"All that God has created in the universe will be involved in the new creation," he said. "It's not just a new heaven, it's a new earth. God has created the beauty of the earth around us. He's given us lovely animals. Look at the immense affection and loyalty of dogs. Look at the beauty of horses. In the new creation, they will not be wasted."

Not for the first time during our conversation, I might have looked perplexed.

"We can't really put it all together," he added cheerfully, "but at the centre of it all is God incarnate. That's enough for me."

As our meeting drew to an end, the table was as strong and stable as ever. The dogs, whose immortality seemed to be assured, had fallen silent, but their owner was still talking with the same enthusiasm and intellectual agility, the same immovable certainty. And I thought again, with the same old doubt, of the long dead soldier and of his last, haunting question: the deepest question of the human heart.

Dining with Benjamin Disraeli

WINIFRED EWING

"Mother was a very dignified person," said Winnie Ewing. "She never seemed to lose her cool. Always patient. I grew up thinking that when I had the time, or when it was a bit easier, I'd be just like her. I used to think about Scarlett O'Hara, who was always going to be like her mother tomorrow. But I never managed it."

"You are less patient than your mother?"

The first lady of Scottish nationalism flashed one of her brilliant smiles.

"A little, yes!"

"Why?"

"I don't know." The smile vanished. "I suppose the experiences I've had have been quite hard."

Now what was this? Some childhood trauma, perhaps?

"Tell me about them."

"Well, the first sojourn in the House of Commons was really ghastly. I was attacked in a way that the Speaker, Horace King, told me no one had been attacked in the history of the House of Commons. It was like a daily crucifixion scene."

"What do you mean?"

"Catcalls every time I went in. Interruptions every time I spoke. Personal insults. Abuse. It's all there in Hansard. That's the beauty of it. It's all recorded for posterity."

Twenty two years after her famous Hamilton by-election victory — the event that prefaced and to a large extent made possible the nationalist bandwagon of the early Seventies — Winnie Ewing spoke of her early experiences as an MP with a bitterness bordering on anguish. The rough and tumble of Westminster life normally leaves few if any permanent scars on the thick skin of the political animal. But in this case, the damage was permanent.

"Who was doing the crucifying?"

"The Labour Party, mostly. The Tories just sat and watched it."

"Were you frightened?"

"Well, it was very nerve-racking. It took every ounce of courage to walk in there every day. But I did it, and I tackled the Prime Minister. Actually, Harold (Wilson) wasn't like that. He was quite kind to me. A lot of them were reasonably kind. But even Bruce Millan made a personal attack on me. I think he was quite sorry afterwards."

"Were people nicer to you behind the scenes?"

"No. That's a fiction about the House of Commons. There aren't a lot of cross-party friendships. I was asked if I would like to join the Liberals' lunch table, which I did sometimes. But on the whole, one sat alone. I remember towards the end, a very nice old man joined me for lunch one day. When he asked me who I usually dined with, I said, 'Oh, I dine with Benjamin Disraeli.' The reason being, I always sat at this little table for two, under a picture of Disraeli."

"You were lonely?"

"Very. But I had the patronage of Emrys Hughes (then Labour MP for South Ayrshire), who was like a father to me. I would have tea with him at five o'clock most days. Of course, he was teased about it. I said to him once, 'Emrys, you're losing your reputation over me.' And he said, 'Oh, lassie, lassie, I lost whatever reputation I had long before you were born!' Unfortunately, Emrys died."

"Apart from the companionship of Emrys Hughes, was there anything that made the experience bearable?"

"Oh, I just felt the whole place was disgusting and obscene. Trial by ordeal. Laughing at cruelty. Cruellest of all when the House was quiet. As Lady Tweedsmuir once put it to me, 'A full House is a fair House.' But if you survived it with dignity, they started giving you a bit of credit. When I went back in 1974, I was really rather well received. I'd got through it. Come out on top, as it were."

"Why did the Labour Party hate you so much?"

"Because I'd won a safe Labour seat."

"As simple as that?"

"Well, it was really the end of the neat carve-up between safe Labour seats and safe Tory seats. My election tended to make the two parties examine their selection procedures for Parliamentary candidates. Suddenly a little bit of talent here and there was necessary, and the John Smiths of this world began to be interspersed with the trade union hacks and the landlords. The late Oliver Brown, who was a very witty man, put it well. He said that when I won Hamilton, you could feel a chill along the Labour back-benches looking for a spine to run up."

Winnie Ewing was born in Glasgow 60 years ago. She went to school — Queen's Park Secondary — not far from where she now lives with her husband Stewart. He is a chartered accountant, she still a practising solicitor in addition to her responsibilities as Euro MP for the Highlands and Islands. We met amid the cheerful clutter of a basement study in her home-cum-office. A secretary escorted me downstairs. Mrs Ewing greeted me warmly and we sat together on a sofa exchanging a few introductory pleasantries.

"How long will this take?" she demanded abruptly as I switched on the tape recorder. The sharp tone took me by surprise.

"Could you spare an hour?"

"I'd rather not. I'm really very busy."

"How about 45 minutes?"

We settled for that.

I already knew a little about Winnie Ewing's childhood, having studied an election leaflet on the reception desk upstairs. I knew, for example, that she had a Highland granny — Jean Stewart from Appin. "Like most Glaswegians," she added, when I asked her about it.

The leaflet had a patriotic Bain cartoon on the front representing Mrs Ewing in her flattering Brussels role as "Madame Ecosse". She certainly has impeccable credentials for the part: not only a Highland granny but a covenanting martyr on her father's side. "We used to go as children to put wreaths on his grave. A kind of ceremony. I didn't think there was anything odd about that. It was only much later I realised it was quite a remarkable thing."

Her father, a cabinet-maker, was badly injured in an accident.

He lost his right hand, and his trade. With the compensation — £500 — he started in business as a wholesale paper merchant.

"Was it a political family?"

"He was an early member of the ILP. Because he was a wee bit better off than some of them — we lived in a three room and kitchen, but it was rather a nice tenement — we used to put up people. I remember we once put up Fenner Brockway. When I got to the House of Commons, Lord Brockway came through to see me and asked me if I was George Woodburn's daughter. Then he turned to the policeman and said, 'I once dangled her on my knee. Do you think she's any the worse for it?'"

Her older sister became active in the socialist club at Glasgow University. Winnie also went to Glasgow University, but chose to join the National Party.

"How did you recognise the SNP as your side?"

"I must say I was influenced by the speeches of John MacCormick (nationalist Rector of the University). I went to hear him and decided he was right — there was no way to get the necessary justice for the people of Scotland or its deserved international participation without going this road. I've never seen any reason to change my mind."

"What did your father think when you joined the SNP?"

"He said I was a traitor to the working class."

"Did he mean it?"

"Oh yes, he said it seriously. 'However,' he said, 'I will continue to pay for your education.' He died on August 8, 1967, three months before I won Hamilton. Among his papers — I'd wound up his estate, such as it was — was a membership card of the Scottish National Party signed July 25, 1967. A friend of mine had been going round trying to get members one sunny summer's evening and recruited my father."

"But your father didn't tell you?"

"No."

"Had you made it up with him?"

"Oh, yes. But he remained critical. He was very addicted to thinking that the Labour Party would give Scotland its dominion status. That had been the policy of the ILP. When it faded away, he always voted for the Labour Party and supported my sister's politics. He hadn't thought it out properly."

"Do you share your father's socialist outlook?"

"Yes. I want to have all public resources nationalised — gas, electricity, water, transport. I'm not very sure about Clause 4. But then, neither is the Labour Party."

When I first met Winnie Ewing in the early Sixties, I knew nothing of her nationalist sympathies. She was at that time merely a hard-working and articulate official of the Glasgow Bar Association who could be relied on to fill the odd spare column of the Glasgow Herald. She seemed happy to give me her association's views on legal matters of the day; I for my part was happy to print them. The relationship only came unstuck when I wrote something that somehow incurred Mrs Ewing's displeasure. She complained to the paper's reclusive Deputy Editor, George MacDonald Fraser, who in turn implored me to get the lady off his back. Mr Fraser's literary ambitions were as unknown to me as Mrs Ewing's politics. Later he emerged from his editorial eyrie with a best-selling novel and disappeared to a tax haven. Mrs Ewing also became famous, though not nearly as rich.

Mrs Ewing did not remind me of our brief working relationship or its untimely end. She has probably forgotten all about it. Even then, however, she had a winning smile and a forceful manner. Three or four years later, I must have been the only person in Scotland who was not in the least surprised by her triumph at Hamilton. But it did surprise me to learn now of the hurt she suffered at Westminster, and still feels.

"Didn't you find that your lawyer's training helped?" Yes, she thought, in the sense that court lawyers were often roughly dealt with by judges. But Emrys Hughes had once told her that she suffered from a great disadvantage being a lawyer in the House of Commons. 'When you stand up to address this House,' he had said, 'you're foolish enough to think that you can persuade your audience. Don't you know that in this House, no one has ever persuaded anyone of anything?'

"Was he right?"

"There was a notable exception...the case of Rosslyn Mitchell, famous Glasgow socialist and most eloquent member, who was said to have persuaded the House in a spur of the moment speech on the English prayer-book. But generally Emrys was right — it's not a place for persuasion. And there are so few really funny MPs."

"Can you think of any?"

"Iain Macleod was funny. Michael Foot, too, before he went on to the front bench. And Ian Mikardo was hilarious. He didn't like me, though."

"You were unhappy at Westminster. Were you any happier about the instant fame in Scotland?"

"I found it very difficult. I didn't like it because it was like being a heroine. When I went to speak all around Scotland as the party insisted I did, I had audiences of hundreds with hundreds more turned away. It was all a kind of nightmare."

"What was wrong with being a heroine?"

"Well, it's very nice for everyone but the person concerned. If you were going into a restaurant with your children, you wondered if they were going to behave, you couldn't hit them or tell them off. I don't think the children liked it either."

"Did they show it?"

"It was very hard when I came back from London on a Thursday night. My little boy, who was only three when I was elected, was very angry with me. 'Where you been?' and 'Why you went?' That was what I got on a Thursday night. Very deadly cross-examination! But then the whole family came down to the House in July and stayed in London for the month. It was so funny. My wee boy thought it was such a great place to play. He went around dressed up as a policeman and they all treated him like a pet. He once wandered into Harold Wilson's room and Harold's press secretary took his photograph."

After her lonely baptism of fire between 1967 and 1970 (Labour regained the Hamilton seat at the general election), Mrs Ewing was in good company when she returned as MP for Moray and Nairn in 1974. The SNP contingent had grown to the size of a football team, and the party's North Sea campaign ("It's Scotland's oil") was at its peak.

"Looking back, wasn't this materialistic approach a mistake?"

"How could it have been? The Labour Party had preached that we were too poor for self-government. The myth had to be destroyed. It was never true, of course. Point for point, we're much wealthier than countries like Switzerland, Norway, Holland or Denmark — that's even without the oil. But the oil was the one thing that completely destroyed the myth, and it had to be done ruthlessly and quickly. You don't hear people saying we're too poor for self-government now. They have to use other arguments."

"All the same, I wonder whether nationalism isn't essentially an emotional thing. What is it for you?"

"Och, it's a mix of all the things it ought to be. It's just a feeling that my country is deprived of a normal experience and is the poorer for being deprived. We're not sitting where the nations meet, we have no influence on the international scene, we're not achieving justice for our people. Also, on occasions, I've found it very depressing to be associated with the immorality of successive British governments."

"What immorality?"

"I'm thinking of when the Labour government supplied arms to Nigeria and for their own reasons didn't stop a war that was unnecessary and could have been prevented. Five million people were killed — the population of Scotland. Nuclear policy is another example. The Falklands war another. And so on. Immoral things in which we become embroiled."

"A lot of SNP supporters seem to detest the English."

Mrs Ewing called that a very nasty myth, and a crazy thing to suggest. Perhaps she had not listened on the radio to the recent xenophobic debate about Scottish nationalism from her own Glasgow University. But she did admit to being offended by English arrogance.

"It's pretty irritating to know that although you're meant to be an equal partner, the land mass is referred to as England and the Queen is referred to as the Queen of England. And when they talk about statistics, they don't make it clear that they're talking only about England and Wales. So many insults like that at so many levels."

"Do the English care whether the Scots stay or go?"

"I don't think it's a burning issue with most of them. When I won Hamilton, there was a great fuss made of me and the people of England were quite upset at the thought we wanted to leave them. But over the years, that's changed. Now most English people would say that if that's what we want, we're perfectly entitled to have it."

"So you've nothing against the English as such?"

"Nothing at all. We just want to be a normal country. Of course, the Scottish politicians are probably the biggest objectors."

"Really?"

"Well, they like going to London. They like it down there."

"Why on earth should they?"

"They like the big pool of patronage. And they're looked after. If they lose their seat, they get a good job. Many of them aren't employable on the labour market, you understand. So they don't want to have a parliament in Scotland. Well, there might be one or two that do. John Smith, I believe, is quite sincere. But basically, most of them like things just as they are."

"You're 60 now. Do you think you'll see an independent Scotland in your lifetime?"

"I think so. I thought it would have come sooner, but I was optimistic. People like Gwynfor Evans (former leader of Plaid Cymru) told me it wouldn't be as easy as I thought. I think the people of Scotland let us down. They lost their nerve."

"You mean the referendum?"

"Not just that. Maybe we should have left the House more than we did, stopped being so insanely anxious not to miss votes. Sometimes we thought we should give the place up and go round Scotland all the time addressing big rallies. But then the Scots are funny about money. There was this attitude that if we were being paid to do a job, we'd better do it."

"Why are you still optimistic?"

"Because we've been down every other road. The Labour Party have broken their promises, the Tories are quite clearly unionists, the CBI and all their pals have betrayed us..."

"The Labour Party say they'll deliver a Scottish Assembly."

Winnie Ewing wasn't having that.

"I'm totally cynical about their promises. I have to be, because my father believed them all his life — and look what happened to him. He died a disillusioned man."

An Attitude of Mind

MAURICE LINDSAY

"You once likened your interest in Scotland to a long drawn out love affair. What stage have you reached in the relationship?"

"I no longer get exasperated," Maurice Lindsay said. "There's a poem of mine in which I finish by describing Scotland as an attitude of mind. By which I mean that I no longer see it as a political entity."

"Tell me about this attitude of mind."

"Well, the Scots feel very passionately that they are a nation, and of course they are. But at the same time, they're a nation that doesn't want to stand on its own feet. They want to sing sentimental songs, they want to get into a great and sometimes lamentable tizz over things like football. They concentrate on the unessentials. They celebrate Burns in a mindless kind of way..."

I thought that was a bit rich coming from one of our leading Burnsians. At our last meeting, we had shared a platform at Alloway Burns Club with the late Lord Ross of Marnock. I was there merely to crack a few feeble jokes, but Dr Lindsay and Lord Willie gave every sign of taking the occasion seriously.

"Aren't you helping to perpetrate this annual blow-out?"

"Yes, but I deplore a lot of the Burns celebrations. I mean, when I go, I'm always trying to place Burns in the evolution of Scottish literature. Not what the average Burns-ite wants."

"How does this approach go down?"

"I get rather puzzled farewells at the end. 'Well, that was very interesting,' they'll say, 'and certainly unusual!' But I simply can't be bothered with all this nonsense people talk about Burns."

"What nonsense?"

"Oh, that if Burns was alive today, he'd be a Scottish nationalist and a freemason and all the rest of the rubbish."

"You think it's largely a sentimental social ritual?"

"I do. Of course the Scots are terribly sentimental generally. This craze for music-hall Scotchery, now translated into television terms, is very strong. Although, unlike Christopher Grieve who maintained that it was a fit subject for all-out attack, I don't think it is. Because if it's all that survives, if it's the real core, you can't destroy it and still have anything left."

As one of the pillars of our post-war literary and artistic establishment — poet, musician, author, administrator, reporter, critic, broadcaster and conservationist, Renaissance Man with a vengeance — Maurice Lindsay is well qualified to assess Scotland's cultural identity. But are we as impoverished as he believes? Are Andy Stewart and the Alexander Brothers, and the many embarrassments of the BBC's Hogmanay show, really all that we can still call our own?

"A lot of Scots seem to want more of a say in their own affairs. Isn't that a hopeful sign?"

"I'm not sure a large number want independence. And in sheer practical terms, I can't see any likelihood of an independent Scotland, as I rather wanted to see when I was younger."

"Why? What's changed?"

"Well, almost every kind of industry of any size has been taken over or merged, and if you haven't got industry working for you, you haven't got an awful lot of money to do conservation or patronise the arts or anything else. Whatever it was that made us in the 19th century lead the world and start industries, we've lost. We now cheer when we can induce the Japanese to come and spend their money on providing us with jobs. Not very admirable."

"Couldn't we model ourselves on the small Scandinavian countries, which are scarcely larger than Scotland and not noticeably richer in natural resources?"

"True, but the small Scandinavian countries don't go around inducing Japanese or American firms to get going, they get their own firms going. There's a certain subservience in the Scottish character. It's always been there. It was there in 1707. But it's got worse. You only have to see the way the business community rushes around whenever there's any suggestion of devolution, telling everybody how much it'll harm them. There is this feeling that we're not strong enough, not good enough, to be on our own. Which is very distressing but it's there — we can't pretend it's not."

As we surveyed the state of the Scottish institutions, his pessimism deepened. When I asked him whether the Church of Scotland should be exerting a more decisive influence in our national life, he dismissed that as a lost cause. And he was contemptuous of the claims made for Scottish education:

"So far as I know, there is no other nation in Europe that does not teach its own national history systematically. The teaching of Scottish literature is very much dependent on the enthusiasm and knowledge of individual teachers, and although in the Higher paper, there is always now a Scottish question, it's not mandatory to answer it. That's incredible. That speaks for itself."

"What about the quality of education in Scotland?"

"I wouldn't know about that. I've always been suspicious of the Knoxian belief quoted by some that Scottish education is better than the English. It seems to me that all education in the United Kingdom is inferior to, say, the French, and we seem to achieve an overall lower standard of literacy."

Though Maurice Lindsay didn't much enjoy his own education at Glasgow Academy, he says it taught him self-reliance and good manners. He devoted himself to literature and music — he hoped to become a professional violinist — but neglected practically everything else. He was awarded 2% in mathematics, prompting the examination board to inquire whether perhaps he had been ill on the day of the exam. His headmaster was able to assure them that the boy was always like that.

"Why didn't you pursue a career in music?"

"I damaged my wrist in an accident."

"You could have taught music, perhaps?

"I wouldn't have liked that. I wouldn't have found it satisfying."

Instead, he wrote about it for the Bulletin, a much-loved, much-lamented Glasgow daily, which belonged to a breed now extinct: the intelligent, middlebrow family newspaper. He was its music critic for 14 years, until the paper folded in 1960.

"How lively was Scotland culturally, compared to today?"

"There's far more going on today. I remember once flying back from London and meeting the lawyer Ian Rodger. When I asked him what he'd been doing, he said, 'Well, we've just been founding a thing called Scottish Opera.' I laughed so inordinately that one of the air hostesses came rushing up to see if I was all right. The idea of a city that would support La Boheme and Faust and not much else actually having its own opera company just struck me as ludicrous."

"What does its success show?"

"What it shows is that if you don't write people's tastes down the way television companies are always doing, you can widen people's imaginative reactions considerably."

"You also wrote about the theatre in Scotland. James Bridie would have been alive when you started..."

"He was. I remember in my capacity as drama critic of the Scottish Daily Mail going to a meeting that Bridie was holding complaining about the treatment the Scottish theatre was getting from the Scottish press. Some laconic fellow beside me said, 'Mr Bridie, it sounds to me as if it isn't criticism you want, it's praise.' 'Yes,' cried Bridie, 'praise, damn you, praise, that's what we want!'"

"What did you make of him?"

"A very interesting character. Difficult man to talk to. Very shy. But a marvellous influence in getting the Scotttish theatre going."

"He's in the nadir of his reputation as a playwright. Nobody performs him. Nobody talks about him."

"But that also happened to Shaw, and in a way Bridie and Shaw are not dissimilar. Both postulate arguments wittily, and that's not fashionable in the modern theatre. But these things go in phases. After all, nobody played Bach for about a hundred years after he died."

"Are you encouraged by the state of the Scottish theatre?"

"As a vehicle for plays in Scots, it has declined. Such Scots as there is tends to be either Glasgow or Edinburgh patois. Mostly Glasgow. That's understandable. And there are more people practising the theatre. Whether what they're practising is any good is another matter. I haven't got much patience with this community drama racket or with anything which suggests that any fool can do it. The only reason for trying to write a fugue or a play is to see how very much better Bach and Shakespeare did it."

* * *

Maurice Lindsay spent his middle years as a broadcaster, initially as one of the BBC's first television reporters in Glasgow, later as programme controller and chief interviewer with Border Television. He was the owner of some of Scotland's better-known bow ties, and an elegant and knowledgeable performer on both radio and television. But in 1967, he had the good sense to get out of full-time broadcasting and became the first Director of the Scottish Civic Trust.

"How that happened was rather curious. I was at one of John Noble's wonderful musical house parties at Ardkinglas. He got hold of me and said, 'Look, my friend Jack Maclay — Lord Muirshiel — is starting up a thing called the Scottish Civic Trust and I want you to apply to be the Director.' I said, 'Good heavens, it's an architect, they want, isn't it?' And he said, 'No, it would be disastrous if it was an architect.' So I applied, and got it, and had the most enormous fun."

"Did you enjoy being an administrator?"

"I have a lifelong dichotomy. My father was an insurance manager, my mother was the daughter of an opera singer in America, so I have two sides to my character. The creative side that needs to be able to get away alone and write books and poetry and so on, and the side that needs some practical thing to do to balance that."

"Was it an uphill battle, teaching the Scots conservation?"

"Twenty five years ago, you had to explain the rationale of conservation, you had to argue the cause before you dealt with the case. Now the climate has changed completely, not just in this country but throughout Europe. And in the last two or three years particularly, there's been an awareness that it isn't just the physical man-made heritage, or the natural heritage, but the total environment — the ozone layer and all the rest of it. Without a shadow of a doubt, if we don't control the philosophy of market values, we will destroy the planet within a measurable space of time. People are now aware of this, and more willing to pay to eradicate the damaging aspects of pollution."

I wondered what had satisfied him most in his professional life: his conservation work, his broadcasting, his poetry — or what? His reply was immediate and emphatic.

"Oh, the poetry. That's the important thing. That's the thing that contains most of me."

"When did you start writing poetry?"

"I was 14. Dreadful stuff. The editor of the Glasgow Academy Chronicle came up with a copy of it the other day and tactlessly sent it to me. I said, 'Burn all copies you can lay your hands on! Immediately!' But I don't know if he will!"

"Why is poetry so important to you?"

"I've always felt the impulse to try to capture the moment that has moved me, delighted me, angered me — in a way that is there for others to share. I've really aimed at celebrating the ordinary stuff that makes up our lives. In fact, the nicest thing ever said about my work was what Christopher Rush wrote in the Scottish Literary Journal — 'He makes the mundane marvellous'."

"You describe yourself as a minor poet. What is the quality that separates the minor from the major?"

"I've only known one or two major poets. One was Hugh MacDiarmid, a major poet for about 5% of his work, the other T.S. Eliot, a major poet for a bit more. Maybe that's not an answer, but there are very few major poets. There are minor poets who think they're major poets and behave as they think major poets ought to behave."

"Which is?"

"Usually rather stupidly and arrogantly."

"What was the 5% of MacDiarmid that made him a major poet?"

"Oh, the early things, the Scots things. A Drunk Man Looks at the Thistle is one of the greatest poems ever written in Scotland, if not the greatest. It embraces and brings to life the whole quality of Scottish life. It has an extraordinary pungency of phrase and intensity of imagery. Remarkable achievement."

"What about the other 95%?"

"Then he had his fall off the bus in London. Among other things, it did something to his sense of balance and rhythm. Almost everything he wrote after that was increasingly dead rhythmically, and he had this terrible desire to pretend to a knowledge that he didn't possess. Great quotations lifted from people's books — I don't know who that was meant to impress."

"Did you like him personally?"

"He was an extraordinary man, the most extraordinary man I've ever met. As C.M. Grieve he was charming, courteous, almost gallant in a slightly old-fashioned sort of way. But as soon as he became Hugh MacDiarmid and picked up a pen, vitriol instead of ink flowed out. And he espoused the silliest causes. The one I really couldn't forgive was his defence of the Russian invasions of Czechoslovakia and Hungary, his declaration that the future belongs to communism. We're already seeing that the future does nothing of the sort."

Maurice Lindsay has lost count of the number of books he has written and edited: about 60, he thinks. They are wide-ranging in theme: from topography to biography, environmental studies to personal reminiscence. He has several more about to roll off the production line — and is hard at work on his collected poems, which he would like to sub-title "1940-1990". He continues as a consultant to the Scottish Civic Trust and is Secretary-General of a conservation body called Europa Nostra which involves a good deal of travel. But still he finds time to listen to music for two hours every day: "my abiding passion, and very necessary to me." He is 71.

"Here you are, past three score years and 10, and still grafting away — almost as hard as ever, it seems to me."

"Well, yes. One old boy said to me, 'My boy' — I was then in my late fifties — 'you know what to do if you want to reach my age? Keep your bowels and your brains open!' Quite right! You can't just sit and look at the roses all day — or, God save us, television."

But the intervention of God, even in the interests of saving him from the box, is not a serious proposition for Maurice Lindsay. He is philosophical about his absence of faith.

"I'm a humanist. Became one at the age of 14. I've never really altered my view."

"Now what does this mean? That you're a non-believer?"

"It means I don't have the foggiest idea. And I'm not prepared to accept highly improbable religious theories."

"Such as?"

"Well, any of them. Catholicism. The Moslem thing. Any of them. If there is a God, He's not going to worry two hoots how they worship. To kill people and torture people and generally display bestial qualities on behalf of religion — a method of worship — is absolutely fatuous."

"What about immortality?"

"Well, I don't expect to go fluttering around in the skies in some endlessly boring way, with all those ghastly people I've spent my time avoiding here. I can think of nothing worse than a hereafter like that."

"What do you expect, then?"

"Nothing at all! Nothing at all!"

He seemed reasonably content at the prospect.

Epitaph for a Civil Servant

SIR WILLIAM KERR FRASER

The Scottish Assembly should have been celebrating its 10th anniversary about now. Apparently they made a nice job of converting the former Royal High School building in Edinburgh into a home for our directly elected legislature. There were endless jokes about President Willie Ross and Prime Minister Winnie.

There was even a senior civil servant waiting patiently in the wings. When William Kerr Fraser was appointed Permanent Under Secretary of State at the Scottish Office in April, 1978, he expected to be running the Scottish Executive — the civil service arm of the Assembly — within 18 months. Then came the referendum.

"Was the result a big disappointment?"

"My view was — still is — that administration in Scotland was like a polo mint. There was a hole in the centre. So to that extent I was disappointed in the outcome of the referendum. But I don't conceal from you that it was also a relief — because if the Assembly had come we would have had a pretty rough time."

"In what way?"

"There was this feeling in Scotland that if only we managed our own affairs, even to the limited extent that the Scotland Act proposed, everything would become much easier and more straightforward. But there was a downside. I don't simply mean the extra expense. There was also bound to be criticism that this or that would have been better done if we'd stuck with the old arrangement. In those circumstances, what was needed in the population at large, particularly among the opinion-formers, was a tremendous conviction in the pit of the stomach. A conviction in favour of change — that it must happen come what may."

In the event, 30% of the population didn't vote at all. The others were split almost equally. So much for conviction.

But was Sir William himself privately convinced?

"The prospectus was flawed, there's no doubt about that. It was flawed because it attempted for political reasons to have the best of all worlds. The case for proportional representation in the Assembly seemed to me to be overwhelming. The case against the maintenance of the Scottish representation at Westminster at the same level — 71 MPs, I think it was then — was very strong indeed. And the assumption that we could indefinitely expect to have a Secretary of State for Scotland round the Cabinet table, as well as an Assembly, was open to pretty formidable challenge, because the Secretary of State was going to be left with a relatively small department."

"Do you think the Assembly idea will come again?"

"It doesn't seem to be an issue at the moment. I know it is the policy of the Labour Party, and Mr Kinnock is said to be committed to it, but my picture is of opinion polarised between independence in Europe and the status quo."

Sir William has a feeling that the nationalist wave rolls up every 20 years or so. In the early Thirties and early Fifties, the winning candidates in Glasgow University rectorial elections stood on nationalist tickets; in the early Seventies, the SNP held 11 seats at Westminster. If this interesting theory is correct, the next big wave is due in the early Nineties, possibly in the wake of the next general election.

"Why did you want the job here?"

The question amused him. For the only time during our talk, his voice rose above a measured monotone.

"Want it?" He laughed drily. At the end of a wood-panelled corridor at Gilmorehill, the Principal and Vice-Chancellor of Glasgow University sat in his modest office facing a clipping from one of the morning papers (another story about cuts in university funding). He has the administratively well-ordered desk of the high-ranking civil servant which he only recently ceased to be. He was jacketless, and sporting a pair of red braces.

"I was asked if I would be interested," he said, "and was shaken by the suggestion. But the idea of coming back to Glasgow was very attractive. It was a challenge — I am not sure I realised just what a challenge. And I suppose it was very flattering. I certainly didn't seek it."

"You were at that stage preparing for a serene retirement?"

"Yes, I was approached when I had just under two years to go in the civil service."

Fifty years ago, the day the Germans invaded Poland, William Fraser, aged 10, was brought by his mother to the steps of Glasgow University. It was never actually stated that if he did well, and Gilmorehill eluded the German bomb, he would one day return as a student. But young William got the message. He did return — in 1946, straight from Eastwood Secondary School.

"What was it like here in that immediate post-war period?"

"The student population was very large. Enormous numbers of ex-servicemen in their demob suits. They were a lot older than students now, of course, and far more experienced. I used to sit in classes alongside men who'd been away in the war for anything up to seven years and had been majors and captains."

"Was it a time of great hope?"

"Well, great changes were being made under the Labour government. I remember going to Christian youth assemblies in Edinburgh, where we listened to serious debates about Christianity and Communism. I found it all a bit overwhelming."

"Because you were so much younger than the others?"

"I had come up from the fifth year at school. And I'd led a pretty sheltered life. For the whole of my first term, I went home at lunchtime. I was actually afraid to go into the University cafeteria. The thought of being in a cafeteria with a tray in front of me and selecting my own meal and paying for it at the end of the counter...I was quite sure I'd arrive with an empty tray and that people would laugh at me. It sounds quite ridiculous, I know."

He was an only child. His father, an insurance man, appears to have been a quiet, reserved soul, who taught at Sunday School and played bowls. He talked more of his mother, who is still alive (aged 90) and whose influence in his life is perhaps unusually large. He told me that when he has to make an important decision, something which is likely to be controversial and public in its implications, he still asks himself how she is likely to react.

Later in the conversation, when I asked him whether his parents had had to make sacrifices to put him through university, I encountered an example of this matriarchal influence. He replied that his mother would not want to see the word "sacrifice" used in this connection.

"What was your parents' ambition for you?"

"I don't know that they had any ambitions for me. The only one I remember being expressed was that I should do well enough at school to come here. In the direct line, nobody in the family had been to university. Very different from the situation today."

"Yes, it seems fairly easy to get to university now."

"Well, I don't know that it's easy, but I do think that middle-class parents almost by implication put their children under greater pressure. I mean, to get to university in my day was an ambition — an objective to be attained. Now for many families it's a standard expectation."

"Do you welcome that?"

"The fact that the proportion of youngsters in higher education is higher is beneficial. It's in the interests of the country. It means more talent being stretched, and the stretching of talent is really what we're about. But it also means that a lot of young people operate under pressure, and feel inadequate if they don't go to university."

Sir William had little to say about his own schooling. Had he been happy at Eastwood Secondary? "I think I was," he replied. He was not much more forthcoming about his teachers.

"What do you think about the decline in the standing of teachers?"

That got him going again.

"It is very worrying, because it's something that no subsequent education can repair. Numbers have got something to do with it. There were many fewer teachers when I was at school. And the teaching profession has brought it on itself, by the militancy of its spokesmen and a lot of its members. It has lost respect."

"Do the Scots care as much about education as they used to?"

"I think we do, still. But it's much more easily available, and there are so many distractions. Then I hear of the sacrifices some of our overseas students make to come here. I met recently a group of

Chinese students, including a married woman who left China when her child was nine months old and who may be here for more than two years without a break. She has accepted that deprivation essentially because of the value she puts on education."

"Are the universities under attack from the present government?"

"I don't know that they're under attack, but ministers are undoubtedly critical, and suspicious of the way they believe the universities shield inefficiences behind their commitment to research. The universities resent this."

"Justifiably?"

"I think it's very simplistic to say that because Napier College or Glasgow College can produce an engineering graduate less expensively than universities, so universities must be less efficient. Universities are shaped in a different way. We are engaged in the business of education, as distinct from specific training for a particular post."

"But there are vocational courses, aren't there? Isn't medicine vocational?"

"I accept that, but we aim within the medical course, and indeed within the general ambience of the University, to create an atmosphere in which people see this stage of their lives as being more than just training for a particular occupation."

"When you were a student here, did you have any idea what you wanted to do?"

"My original intention was to become a town clerk. From what little I knew, I thought that might be an attractive occupation. So when I finished my arts degree, I followed it with an LLB and was indentured as an apprentice. I came up here for a class at 8.30 in the morning, went to the office at 9.30, then back here for two more classes at four o'clock. As well as being a legal apprentice and a law student, I was president of the SRC and, in order to find some cash to take my girl friend to dances, taught economics in Paisley one day a week."

His early difficulties in the cafeteria were now behind him.

It was during his three years in the RAF that he began to have doubts about returning to the legal profession. He contemplated a career in industry and decided that an outlay of £4 to enter the civil service competition would be a useful investment. He told himself that although he wouldn't be selected, he would learn a lot: most prospective employers modelled their interviewing techniques on the civil service. In fact, he came first equal that year (1955).

"I was absolutely staggered. I had never really thought about the civil service because it seemed to be an occupation reserved for those with very distinguished academic records and largely the preserve of Oxford and Cambridge."

"Were you interested in politics?"

"From the age of 13 or 14 I had been interested in the constitution — the procedures for the making of laws."

"But not party politics?"

"No. If you feel tremendously deeply about political issues, that can be an obstacle in the civil service. A passionate person over a whole range of issues — one issue is not sufficient, as it were, to disqualify — would find the climate difficult. Which is not to say that civil servants are without passion."

These careful distinctions were proving somewhat elusive. I asked Sir William for an example.

"If, for instance, you are a unilateralist, if that's the one issue on which you feel passionately, the civil service would have no difficulty in ensuring that you wouldn't find yourself in any post where a conflict of loyalties might arise."

"Did you have a particular passion?"

"I don't think so. But I would have liked people to be less cynical about government and the processes of government. I would have liked on my gravestone the words: 'He simplified things a little'."

"Will they appear?"

"They will not!"

The Gross Materialist

MICK McGAHEY

In Edinburgh during the Festival, there was at least one haven where it was possible to escape post-alternative comedians, London critics and poets with egg on their ties. This was the SOGAT Club in Brunswick Street, which my taxi driver warmly recommended. "Been there a couple of times," he said. "Good pint and not too expensive." I urged him to take me with all speed.

It was here that I had arranged to meet one of the older turns on the Scottish stage, a far-out fringe performer who at the height of his dramatic powers was capable of extinguishing every light in the land.

The SOGAT Club was nicely bare and functional, as all self-respecting trade union clubs should be. There was a poster in the hall advertising a bingo night. In the lounge, amidst a few glum-looking graphic and allied tradespersons, sat the unmistakable figure of Mick McGahey. The sometime leader of the Scottish miners, when there were still some Scottish miners to lead, was relaxing with a half pint of beer, a whisky, and a copy of the Morning Star.

We retreated to a far corner, and talked about the origins of his lifelong class struggle. He was born in the Lanarkshire mining village of Shotts, which has also produced the singer Bill McCue, the Labour politician Peggy Herbison and the irrepressible journalist Jim Rodger, as well as the best pipe band in the world; it is possibly the only village in industrial Scotland with its own theatre.

"You come from mining stock?"

"Son of a miner. My father was an activist in the 1926 strike. Like many others, he was victimised by the Shotts Iron Company. We finished up in Kent. Quite interesting...the last colliery in Kent was announced for closure this morning."

The Morning Star was full of it. '1,400 pit jobs lost', it announced — alongside 'Ambulances in 999 crisis', 'Unions set for ballot for action', 'Two more cabin crew sacked by BA bosses', 'Aberdeen journalists vote to continue strike', 'Filipino crew unpaid — union', and — the most drastic measure of all, perhaps — 'Vodka and tonics frozen'. I was glad to note that the Morning Star fighting fund was still going strong, £357.05 having arrived in the previous day's post.

"Did you have brothers and sisters?"

"Three brothers, including one who died when I was only months old, and a sister. I've only my sister left."

When Mick McGahey was eight, the family returned to Scotland and settled in Cambuslang. His two brothers went to work at the local pit — Gateside — and Mick followed them in 1939.

"What age were you?"

"Fourteen. Left school on the Friday, was down the pit on the Monday. I was a pony driver when I started. Hard, brutal work. Pick and shovel. As the Reid Report put it in 1944, the mining industry in Britain was the most backward mining industry in the whole of Europe. The coal owners took the profits, but they didn't invest."

"Are you sorry you didn't get the chance to further your education?"

"Oh, yes." He coughed harshly, as he did quite often. "But I wasn't compelled to leave the school or go underground. I wanted to. One thing my father always insisted on was reading. I never went to bed without Jack London. Then Upton Sinclair. And in the Communist Party, there was a very good education system. We went to classes."

"What kind of man was your father?"

I expected Mick McGahey to express some judgement about his father's temperament or character. Instead, he defined him — as he defined the rest of his family — according to politics or religion.

"Oh, very active. He was a foundation member of the Communist Party, and exerted a tremendous influence on me. My two brothers were also members of the party. My sister, no — she was a devout Catholic. As was my mother."

"Your father wasn't a Catholic?"

"No, no. He was what you term an old-time atheist! He wasn't anti-religious, he respected people's religion, but he was what he used to call a gross materialist. But not in the materialistic sense!"

"You were poor?"

"There were no rich miners. The weekly wage of the miner in the 1930s was 50 bob for six days a week, and sometimes you didn't get six days a week, you only got three. You could depend on it that on the Thursday night there was nothing left in the cupboard. My mother used to say, 'This is the day before tomorrow.' And yet it wasn't cruel, brutal poverty. Not the grinding poverty of colonial peoples, or anything like that. But it was poverty all the same. The north ward in Cambuslang had the highest tuberculosis rate in western Europe — including Franco's Spain, as we always used to emphasise."

His mother — a Derry woman — was buried with the blessings of the Roman Catholic Church and the full dignity of a requiem mass. His father had a secular funeral; Jimmy Reid, then Scottish Secretary of the Communist Party, performed the oration.

"Wasn't there ever political conflict between the two sides of the family?"

"No conflict. We paid homage to both their ideals. In fact, my mother supported most progressive causes, as many Catholics do. She supported tenants' movements. She was a member of the Co-operative Women's Guild."

Mick McGahey became active in the Young Communist League, joining the party at the age of 18 just as his father and brothers had before him. But his career at Gateside was short-lived. He was sacked for leading an unofficial strike during the war.

"Do you regret having done that?"

"Yes, it was wrong. The war against fascism was the most important thing at that stage, in the interests not only of Britain but of the international working-class. But I was young, obviously immature, not well-developed politically."

He got a job in the Lothians coalfield and worked there for the rest of the war. His activism, though now tempered by realism, continued more or less unabashed. He campaigned successfully to have an over-crowded miners' hostel closed, came into contact with the Scottish miners' leaders for the first time, began climbing the union hierarchy. And he went on taking famous left-wing philosophers to bed with him.

"What was it about communism that attracted you?"

"The gleam of a socialist future."

"What's that?"

He gave a long prescription for what sounded like Utopia: the ending of poverty, of racial discrimination, of war itself; the creation of a just, equitable society; all that, plus a better standard of living, better education, better working conditions, longer holidays, etc. etc.

"It's a pretty tall order, this gleam."

"It's all the benefits that we don't see in a...well, they call it a market-orientated society now. We called it a capitalist society."

"Have you been to the Soviet Union?" I was curious to know whether Mr McGahey had found anything resembling Utopia in the homeland.

He had been several times.

"And?"

"It's like every other country. I've seen good and bad in it. I've seen things I didn't accept."

"Such as?"

"I've seen working conditions I didn't like in Soviet mines. I've seen women doing heavy manual work on railway lines. Of course, the answer you get is, 'Please remember, we lost 20 million in the second world war. There's a tremendous labour shortage.' But I've also seen Soviet health resorts run by the unions, and Soviet miners enjoying holidays that would have been unbelievable to British miners until quite recently. So, there are weaknesses, yes. But strengths, too, in the social fabric."

It was not a description of Utopia, but it seemed a pretty fair answer.

"Has nothing shaken your confidence in communism?"

"My confidence in communism, and in the Communist Party of Great Britain, has never been shaken."

"What about Hungary?"

"Yes, yes, but in 1956 the Soviet Union was seen as being under threat by counter revolution. Hungary, remember, was a fascist country during the second world war and this was only 11 years after the war."

"What about Czechoslovakia?"

"In 1968 I opposed the Czechoslovakian intervention. I refused to accept the Soviet analysis."

"Has being a communist made life personally unpleasant for you?"

"I've had difficulties," he said cheerfully, knocking back his Scotch. "Over Hungary, for instance. Oh my, yes! Some rough times!"

"How rough?"

"It's not the first time I've been knocked off a platform. Or had the occasional boot put in. Or been threatened in pubs."

When Mick McGahey entered the mining industry, there were 900,000 miners in Britain. Now the total is 100,000 and falling. Of these, only 3,000 are employed in Scotland.

"A tragedy," he called it. "Of course, we could never maintain a manpower of that size. But there's been a terrible destruction of the assets of the industry. And now they're talking about handing what's left back to private ownership..."

In 1974, when I first met him, it all looked quite different. Then he was full-time president of the Scottish miners, a bogeyman of the right-wing press, and a force to be reckoned with. Then miners could still bring down governments. The coal strike in the early weeks of that year made Edward Heath go to the country to fight an election on the question, "Who governs Britain?" Mr Heath lost.

During that strangely exhilarating period, as the lights went out, industry worked a three-day week and television closed down at 10 o'clock, Mick McGahey was cast as the hard man of the NUM compared to the more emollient Joe Gormley. Every other day he chaired crowded press conferences at the union's Scottish headquarters, just around the corner from where we sat now. He was the person I interviewed most often for the BBC. I used to ask him if he saw himself as a threat to democracy.

But when history repeated itself in 1984, it did so as farce. Mr McGahey was still playing second fiddle, but this time to a stubborn Yorkshireman called Arthur Scargill.

"Do you think Mr Scargill handled the strike badly?"

"Arthur did what he was asked by the miners. There were

weaknesses, but that wasn't Arthur Scargill's fault. It was a collective weakness."

"What was it?"

"We under-estimated the determination of this Tory government to destroy the union. They weren't successful, but they very nearly did it. And unlike 1974, we didn't win the public's sympathy as much as we should have done. We were looking on mass meetings as mass movements, but they're not the same thing."

"What's happened since the strike?"

"Well, Arthur's isolated himself to some extent. All he says now is, 'You must take action, else your pit will close.' But he's got to make a wider appeal to the trade union movement. He's got to recognise that it isn't as easy to organise against pit closures."

"Why isn't it?"

"Redundancy payments. We never anticipated the effect of them, and how they've weakened the struggle. I remember using the slogan — we've all used it — 'It's not your job to sell, it's your son's job, it belongs to a future generation.' But then you offer a lad £25,000-£30,000 and his wife starts pressuring him, and you tell him he's got till Saturday to make a decision..."

"The system's breaking up," I suggested. "There isn't really a working class left to defend."

"Oh yes, there's a working class. I still retain the old definition of class as your relationship to the means of production. There are people who hire. There are people who are fired."

"It's not as simple as that any more."

"Not nowadays," he agreed. "There are people who would deny they're working class."

"That's what I mean. The system's breaking up."

"Well, you can't see the fight in the traditional terms. If we had a Labour government, I don't think Neil Kinnock would annul the legislation that compels pre-strike ballots."

"What do you think of Mr Kinnock?"

"He's doing an excellent job. I always say to people, 'It's not hard, but he and Norman Willis are the best leaders we've had when you consider some in the past.' Oh, yes. Big improvements."

"On whom?"

"Kinnock is a big improvement, for instance, on a Callaghan or a Wilson, who were political...Och well, they were adventurers.

They hadn't really a socialist understanding, nor were they close to the movement. They were manipulators."

Mick McGahey has been retired for two years. He says he is happy. He has been catching up on his reading and enjoys caravaning in Blyth, where he meets his old mining pals from Northumberland. His wife and daughter have, he says, conned him into visiting Disneyland, the market-orientated society writ large. Only one thing makes him sad, and that is to pass his former office in Hillside Crescent, where we will never again gather to hear Mick McGahey thunder against the iniquities of a Tory government. The old place is up for sale.

"Now it's down to what...two pits?"

"Well, three. One mothballed. Then Frances and Longannet."

"It's not just an industry that's gone, is it?"

"Of course not. The miners' gala used to be the biggest event in the calendar of the Scottish Labour movement. Will there ever be another? Then take the mining communities. Where will we get our brass bands, our pipers, our choral groups? Mining wasn't just about the extraction of coal. It was the development of a whole culture. That's gone."

When I asked casually towards the end of our conversation whether religion interested him — I was thinking again of his mother's devout Catholicism and wondering whether any of it had rubbed off — I received a surprising answer.

"I left religion when I was very young," he said, "but I've a tremendous number of friends in the religious world. Canon Kenyon Wright (of Scottish Churches House) I would count as a close personal friend. Hugh Ormiston, the Church of Scotland chaplain at Longannet, is another. And I attend the General Assembly every year."

"You do?"

The thought of Mick McGahey with his Morning Star upstairs in the Assembly Hall observing the deliberations of the ministers and elders was instantly implausible.

"I think the Church of Scotland is one of the most democratic churches in existence. Look how they tackled Maggie Thatcher last year! And the work they do in the Church and Nation Committee is tremendous. What I say is this — let Christians and communists come together and there'll be a whole host of things they can agree and act on."

"But I take it that belief in God is not one of those things?"

"I have no belief. But I respect people who do believe."

"And after you're dead — that's it?"

"As far as I'm concerned, yes. That's why it's important to make your contribution down here. In the most positive sense possible."

"Just like your father, then? A gross materialist?"

"That's right!" He laughed throatily, and I asked him if he would like something to drink. He said he would like a wee Bell's.

While I was at the bar, a young man just back from Australia told Mick that he and his father had worked together in the pits in 1943. They entered into an animated exchange about old football teams and the results of memorable games in a braver, more combative past.

"Does he like water in his whisky?" I asked the barmaid.

"No' very much," she said.

Like his communism, Mick McGahey's whisky is fundamentally undiluted.

The Name on the Door

RIKKI FULTON

As I arrived at Josie's place, Francie was just leaving. "I want you to be happy," Josie was saying. Francie, who was carrying a shopping bag, didn't look happy. He rarely does.

For those few readers unfamiliar with one of the great double acts of the Scottish variety stage, I should explain that Francie and Josie are Glasgow teddy boys also known as Jack Milroy and Rikki Fulton. William Hunter observed — in Scottish Theatre magazine, January 1970 — the essential nature of this comic phenomenon:

> Josie (Rikki Fulton), all sharp, quick, tense, likes the taste of big words in his mouth so long as he is allowed to get them wrong. Francie (Jack Milroy), his face sad and crumpled as an unmade bed, doesn't know any words, especially small ones, like work. How on earth did they team up? They are muckers, that's all, mates, friends. One at a time each would be unbearable. But they make sense by the pair like silly kippers, which they also are. They last better than fish, though, because their patter has a time-resistant batter round it to keep it fresh. But dated, yes: nothing much a man, or even a brace of them, can do about that. They have been pickled in their prime — the time of Elvis and D.A. hair cuts and thick-soled shoes...

Twenty years on, the batter is as time-resistant as ever. When the silly kippers made a rare television appearance recently, most of Scotland watched admiringly. And the day I turned up on the doorstep, they were discussing their forthcoming season at the Glasgow King's. Before he was gone, Francie even managed a small, brave smile, possibly at the thought of the advance receipts.

Francie and Josie are pushing it a bit now. Rikki Fulton, the younger of the partners, has just passed his 65th birthday and calls himself a senior citizen. He lives with his second wife, Kate Matheson, in the sort of spacious, comfortable villa that he dreamt of as a child. Unlike Josie, he has come up in the world.

However, Josie would have felt quite at home in his creator's original habitat.

"You're a Glasgow man?"

"I'm an East Ender. Born in Appin Road, Dennistoun — you can't get a more Scottish name for a street than that. Left there when I was three, and went posh. Up to the Riddrie corporation housing estate."

"That was posh?"

"Oh, really quite up-market, then."

"Tell me about Appin Road."

"Grey tenements. I've a great affection for tenements. Nowadays they're just the most wonderful apartments you can buy. But Appin Road was rather different, because it was a room and kitchen. The curious thing is that years later, I could remember every detail of the kitchen almost to the last ornament. I was brought into the world in that room — in the kitchen bed — the recess."

"What do you remember about your mother?"

"I remember her very clearly, though she's been dead a long time. Four feet eleven and a half inches in her shoes. Tiny wee soul. I remember her in the kitchen, standing on the bed — actually on the bed — in a red dressing gown. Quite distraught, really in a very bad way. I think I was responsible for her nervous breakdown."

"You were a bad baby?"

"No. But I was born when my mother was 40. Highly significant! Here she was, a middle-aged lady, embarrassed at having produced another child and convinced that people were looking at her strangely and whispering to each other. Classic psychosis. She was of a particular generation who did not recognise the existence of the sexual act. My mother never used the word sex. She used the word Men with a capital M. 'I don't like Men,' she would say. We all knew what she meant. And yet she had the greatest sense of humour."

"She enjoyed a joke?"

"Loved jokes, especially when they were slightly risque." Mr Fulton thought about that, and corrected himself. "Maybe slightly vulgar would be a better definition."

"What's the difference?"

"Possibly sexual jokes might come under the heading of risque. Vulgar jokes have to do with bodily functions. But she, of course, never quite grasped their meaning. The whole family would be laughing uproariously, while my mother was still struggling with the tag. Then, later, there would be a screech from her room and hysterical laughter..."

"The penny had finally dropped?"

"And the whole family would go to my mother's room, and we would enjoy the joke all over again."

"What does that tell you about the nature of comedy?"

"It underscores the maxim that a joke is not a joke until an audience has laughed at it!"

"It's a question of timing?"

"Basically, yes. But personality is also incredibly important. One of the essential things about making people laugh is that first of all, you've got to make them like you. If they don't like you, they won't laugh. That's why it's often very difficult for two men to make their living as a double act and why so many of the great double acts end up at loggerheads. Because there are two of them out there, fighting for the one love — the one adulation."

This sad but perceptive comment set Mr Fulton speculating about the personal instability of comedians and the curious fact that so many have what he called "difficulties over relationships". He reeled off the names of half a dozen celebrated comics with unhappy private lives, and had difficulty naming one (apart from his own partner, Jack Milroy) who has a stable marriage. He finally selected Jimmy Tarbuck.

"Why is this?"

"It's got something to do with what you have to do when you're faced with a career in comedy, when you make your living putting your emotions on the line."

"It's true, then, that comics are very insecure people? That comedy is a form of self-defence?"

"It certainly was in my case. I was the youngest of three boys — by a long way. Within the family, I was referred to as 'the baby', or 'the kid', or 'him'. I came into a family that was established, where there was an eight-year-old and a 14-year-old, and a mum and dad who obviously regarded themselves as having finished with that part of their lives. I was an outsider — an interloper. I was 32 before I became absolutely convinced that I was a blood relative of these people."

"Truly?"

"Oh, I was quite convinced I'd been discovered on a doorstep."

"What happened at the age of 32?"

"I suppose I'd matured as much as I was going to, and had thought it through. And facially, I was beginning to resemble my elder brother."

It occurred to me that throughout a long, detailed and vivid recollection of his early life, Rikki Fulton had not once mentioned his father. When I expressed some surprise about this, he invited me to draw the obvious conclusion.

"My father," he said, "was the quietest man I've ever known in my life. He never spoke to me, except to tell me to stop playing the piano, and that in somewhat colourful terms."

"What did he do?"

"He was in Singer's. A very clever locksmith. He could open any door. Then he became a shopkeeper."

"It was a typical Glasgow family, then?"

"Yes, a matriarchal society. She was the ruler. She made the decisions. It was my mother who took me to the hospital when I was near death — I had a tubercular gland which just about did for me. My mother who went up to the school and told the teachers to lay off her child."

"You didn't get on well at school?"

"If only I'd had the thirst for knowledge that I gained after leaving school, if only I'd had the audacity — the bottle — to say, 'Excuse me, sir, I don't understand that, would you be good enough to explain that again?', I think I would have got on a lot better. English I sailed through. And I once got 100% for art."

At the start of our meeting, Kate Fulton had asked hospitably when it might be suitable to bring tea. After an hour, perhaps? Yes, an hour sounded fine. By then, I judged, we would be nearing the end of the interview — via her husband's first professional engagement with the BBC in Glasgow, his many pantomimes, his Five Past Eight seasons, his Scotch & Wry television series, his film appearances, his recollections of people and events.

The charming Kate arrived on cue with a glorious afternoon tea served from a tiered cakestand. But our interview had not gone according to plan. We had still not progressed from Mr Fulton's fascinating childhood. We were spiritually stuck in Appin Road.

"When did you leave school?"

"When I was 15. I got a job in a builder's merchant's office at 134 St Vincent Street. A one-man business with a double office and a name on the door. I've often dreamt about that office. Always with the name on the door. Some special attachment. Something to do with identity. It seemed to say what you are...who you are..."

"Is that still important to you?"

"Yes. I adore letterheads, for example. I'm a stationery freak."

Mr Fulton's own letterhead has his address in ornate lettering across the full length of a finely woven A-4 sheet.

"You have a problem about your identity," I suggested obviously.

"I do?"

He sounded surprised and intrigued, though not displeased. We had with some relish already devoured the more mouth-watering contents of the lowest tier of the cakestand, and were now eyeing the various dainties above.

I persisted: "Well, yes. Lonely child. Brothers much older than yourself, uncommunicative father, dominant mother..."

"I think that's right," he said, warming to the theme. "But what I discovered was that when I made the family laugh, I felt secure. That was fine. But when they were not laughing, I was quite insecure. And really rather afraid."

"And that remained true, did it — when you became a comedian?"

"It's a long, long time since I faced a hostile audience of any kind. But I did once have difficulty getting across to an audience — I think because of my own personal circumstances at the time. They were not laughing. What they were saying to me was, 'We don't like you.'"

"You were unhappy then?"

"Well, my first marriage was up the spout. Yes, a difficult time."

"We're jumping ahead. What happened after the builders' merchants with the name on the door?"

"I became a customs clerk. Loved that, except it was a stressful situation in one way. If you made a mistake, it was almost considered to be criminal — and they fined you! There was a woman there called Miss Flynn. She sat behind an old-fashioned high desk. Probably the ugliest woman I ever saw in my life. Very red face, a great beak, glasses, hair scraped back. And next to her, this man — equally unpleasant, Germanic looking, with as pale a face as hers was red. I think they were having a sort of...well, I'm going to use the word affair. But that has the wrong connotations."

"Miss Flynn and you didn't get on?"

"She was like a really awful headmistress. She would rant and rave. 'Stupid boy!' she would cry. It was hands behind the back time. Literally."

The appalling Miss Flynn was not the only source of adolescent dread. When Chamberlain returned from Munich with his meaningless piece of paper, at least one inhabitant of the Riddrie corporation housing estate felt a tingle of fear.

"When the war started, it seemed that every boy I knew was going into Fighter Command, and making noises like aeroplanes. I must be honest, I couldn't understand that. I just didn't want to know about war. There was nothing heroic about me at all. Suddenly, a wee girl I fancied very much — all the girls were absolutely enthralled at the thought of these boys going to fight for king and country — this wee girl said to me, 'What are you going to do?' I felt I couldn't say, 'I'm not going to go. I'm a conscientious objector.' Well, I don't suppose I was anyhow. With me, it was just cowardice."

"So what did you say to her?"

"Out came this voice with an explanation I'd never heard before. I was going to join the Navy. 'Why?' she said. 'Well,' I said, 'I'm in a shipping office, and I know all about shipping.' Strangest reason!"

He promptly volunteered, and joined up on his 18th birthday. His experiences in the Navy, though harrowing, proved rewarding in later life. They provided the inspiration for one of the richest themes in his work: the caricature of the Scottish working-class lad hopelessly aping southern manners.

"I remember when I was commissioned. The first question they asked was what your father did. Then education. On guard duty one night, the guy next to me suddenly wanted to know what school I'd been to. 'Whitehill,' I said — deliberately disguising the fact that it was just a Glasgow secondary. I became terribly conscious of background — social standing. In some cases, they even taught you how to use a knife and fork. Sent you away to learn manners!"

But there was nothing in the school of Navy etiquette to prepare him for the moment when his ship was torpedoed. He spent five hours in the waters of North Africa before he was picked up. He saw his skipper dead on the deck.

"It wasn't the sight of his body that upset me, but the fact I'd seen his wife with him just a few weeks before. She must have boarded at Greenock or somewhere. That's what I find so obscene about death. It's not the dying or the being dead. It's the wrenching apart..."

"Are you a religious man?"

"A couple of years ago, I went into hospital for a simple operation and the doctors found something they didn't know was there — this tumour. I could have bled to death on the operating table. Both Katy and I were atheists I suppose, but because of what happened to me, we both took another look at it. I saw an opportunity perhaps to return to a faith, and be happier for it."

"Where did that lead you?"

"Katy's taken it a good deal further. But then she's a very special lady. She's how I see the Christian — goes out of her way to help people, feels for them, cares for them in a way that frankly I don't. We became members of the Church, and I found I liked going to Church. Enjoyed it. Liked being with people who believed. And I read and read all sorts of books, and talked to some very interesting people. Oh, the debate is wonderful. I adore the debate."

"But you haven't reached a conclusion?"

"Yes, I have."

"What is it?"

"I just can't accept. Or — if there is an alternative — that it's just too difficult. And the Church of Scotland message is pretty downward-looking, I think."

"In what sense?"

"Well," he said regretfully, "you don't really get a sense of joy and good news, do you?"

At which I thought inevitably of the annual Hogmanay ritual on our television screens: of the doom-laden Scottish minister created by Mr Fulton, who hilariously fills the fag end of the year with his deeply lugubrious reflections on Life.

"Ah!" I announced triumphantly. "You're talking about the Reverend I.M. Jolly!"

But Rikki Fulton wasn't laughing.

The Common Touch

MOST REV. THOMAS WINNING

As a student for the priesthood, the future Archbishop of Glasgow was once confronted in an exam paper by a moral dilemma close to home. Was fiddling the system ever justified? "When I came out," said Tom Winning, "I went round the others to see how they'd answered the question. I discovered I was the only one who'd argued that in certain circumstances it was quite just to do it."

"What circumstances?"

"If you were not getting enough to live on anyway."

The leader of Glasgow's 280,000 Roman Catholics was born into the poverty of small-town industrial Lanarkshire. His father, a former miner and steel worker, lost his job during the depression of the Thirties and was unemployed for 15 years. One day, someone suggested to Mr Winning that making sweets would be a way of passing the time.

"Well, he got into this in a really big way. He used to buy bags and bags of sugar from the Co. And he would go round the shops and offer his sweets for sale."

"What kind of sweets?"

"All sorts of tablet and boilings. Even got to the stage of marzipan walnuts. They were the luxury items. Of course there was a means test at the time. He went to them and he said, 'I'm making these sweets. What do I do?' And they told him he could make four shillings profit a week — that would be legitimate. The parish priest told him to make as much as he could!"

"And did he?"

"Oh, he never made a fortune or anything like it. He did it mainly just to keep himself occupied. He used to say, 'My only ambition is to educate my two children. Once I've done that, I'll stop it.' Well, my sister graduated as a teacher and the following year, I became a priest. They came out to Rome for that. When they got back, my father never made another sweet."

"What kind of character was he?"

"He was very, very even-tempered. I met a man the other day who said, 'I worked beside your father when I was 16 years of age, and he gave me a belling off for swearing. I've never used a bad word since.' The more mature I got, the more I appreciated the integrity of the man, you know?"

"What about your mother?"

"A very good manager. I never knew I was poor. I was as well dressed as anybody in the community. The only thing was, we never got a holiday. I remember the folk next door always went to Portobello for a week. Came back with whelks! When I asked my mother whether we could go on holiday too, she said, 'All right, we'll go next year...provided you are willing to eat margarine every day instead of butter.' I told her to forget it."

"At least you had the sweets to enjoy."

"When we went to see my mother's aunt, she used to give us half a crown and tell us to buy sweets from daddy. I thought, 'That'll be right. If we want them, we'll take them!'"

Tom Winning was brought up in a devoutly religious household. His father was a voluntary worker for the Catholic charity, the Vincent de Paul Society, which looked after the poor. In Craigneuk, a deprived parish between Wishaw and Motherwell, there were many families worse off than the Winnings.

In the foyer of the Archbishop's splendidly refurbished offices overlooking the Clyde, I had bought a copy of Flourish, the newspaper of the Archdiocese. The main item on the front page was about poverty in the West of Scotland and the Church's urgent concern for the welfare of deprived families. It appeared that little had changed. But could the poverty of the late Eighties be likened to the poverty of the Thirties?

"It's a different kind of poverty. You might go into a house and find wall to carpets. Comfortable in that way. But you'll also find that the family aren't eating. Look at the youngsters. The government first got the idea of school meals in 1917, when the physique of young men going into the Army was so abominable. They swore they would feed the nation once the war was over. Well, it took them 20 years to do it. But now kids are going home in the middle of the day to junk food, not to anything worthwhile."

"When did you decide to become a priest?"

"It was just the natural thing to do. As a boy I'd been very much involved in the parish. I became an altar boy, which meant I was there every morning, serving mass, before I went to school. I must have been about 13 when I spoke to our parish priest about it."

"So there was no single event that made up your mind?"

"No. It was really a desire to be the same as they (the priests) were. To look after people."

"You went to a Catholic secondary school in Motherwell. Did you like that?"

"I wasn't all that enamoured of it. If you were academically good, people were interested in you, if you weren't...." The Archbishop left the sentence unfinished. "I was probably glad to get shot of it all."

"But you're a vociferous supporter of the separateness of Catholic education."

"Oh yes, there's a tremendous influence exercised by teachers who share the same values as your parents. Catholic schools aren't perfect. There are failures. But even today I am constantly amazed and comforted when I go to a school and come across the commitment of these folk. Teachers in general are a first-class bunch of people, whether they're Catholic or not."

"If that's the case, what's so wrong with non-denominational schools?"

Archbishop Winning wasn't falling for that one. "They don't have the same religious commitment, that's what's wrong. Otherwise it would be much easier to get teachers in the non-denominational sector to teach religion. You might have four or five teachers willing to teach it in a school of 1,000 pupils."

"Hasn't segregated education made religious intolerance in the West of Scotland a good deal worse?"

"That's a right old hairy one! There's bigotry in Edinburgh. There's bigotry in Perth. But they don't get away with it in the West of Scotland!"

"If Catholic and Protestant children were educated together," I persisted, "there would be less prejudice."

"There'd be less religion."

"There'd be less prejudice."

"I don't know. Is the prejudice growing or diminishing?"

"Well, I know you're a football fan. The reaction of the more blue-nosed Rangers supporters to the signing of Mo Johnston doesn't suggest it's diminishing."

"The older I get, the more convinced I am that the prejudice is what Billy Connolly calls a hobby. It doesn't go deep. Well, maybe it does with some. But mostly it's a laugh. A joke. The Mo Johnston thing is the best thing that could have happened."

"Well, yes. But the reaction to it in the West of Scotland has confirmed the English in their opinion that, underneath the glossy new Glasgow image, it's the same old divided community."

"Surely not. If the reaction was only verbal, we should be damned thankful. What would we have got 50 years ago? Over the piece, things are much better than they were when I was a boy. And you can't blame the Catholic schools. They're there to teach the Christian faith."

"From a specifically Catholic standpoint."

"Ah, but the dogmas are not that different. They are to preach Jesus Christ, to preach Love Your Neighbour. Yes, we are dealing with a community that's split. I'm not denying that. But it would be an awful lot worse if we couldn't give our children some really strong religious beliefs to enable them to cope with what they're going to face later on."

"What is the origin of the split?"

"The Catholics have never been in the majority. The power has been with the native Scots who resented greatly the Irish coming over here and stealing their jobs. We've never been able to get rid of that. I mean, where in the wide world do you get so much anti-Catholic feeling as you get in Scotland?"

"Ah. So now you're saying that it really isn't a joke."

"I think the football business is a joke. And there's a goodwill now that was never apparent before. But there are still many non-Catholics in Scotland who would rather see their kids dead than see them become a Catholic."

"As bad as that? Even today?"

"I can think of two people just now who've been driven to insanity by the treatment they got from their families."

In three and a half months of interviews, I never heard a more depressing statement than that.

The Most Reverend Thomas Joseph Winning conforms to few people's preconceptions of an Archbishop. His accent and conversational style are workaday West of Scotland; he has about him an informality and common touch that are instantly disarming; he looks and sounds like an artisan. If this is fairly unusual in the Christian hierarchy, it is not without an outstanding precedent.

He is also extraordinarily youthful. Aged 64, he might pass for a man in his late forties. Is this, perhaps, an advertisement for a life of celibacy and goodness? If so, it is not one that carries much appeal in the modern world. According to Flourish, only one priest would be ordained in the Archdiocese of Glasgow in 1990.

"Why this decline in vocations?"

"I think celibacy is a very strong reason. Probably offputting."

"Was it tough for you to accept?"

"It would be wrong if I said it was easy. If you're normal, you go through life seeing it as quite a cross. I think I'm normal."

He had spent some time on the telephone trying to arrange a video camera for his grand niece's first birthday party. I sensed that he was looking forward to this occasion immensely.

"So you've sometimes thought it would be good to have children of your own?"

"No doubt about that. But you're prepared to forgo it if you can give your love and affection to a community of people rather than to a single person or two or three."

"Apart from celibacy, are there other reasons for the reluctance of young men to enter the priesthood?"

"It's to do with the type of society we're living in. There's so much emphasis on material things that religion isn't all that fashionable."

"You're saying that people don't need God any more?"

"Aye. They've cracked open most of the mysteries of the universe. Sex without babies. Babies without sex. Man on the moon. Going to Mars. Satellites. Costa del Sol. Small families."

"That's quite a list. What's wrong with small families?"

"Nothing," said the Archbishop, "if only they were a bit bigger. Did you hear that girl athlete yesterday? She kept talking about 'numero uno'. That's the one that matters now."

"The church was very good at helping people to cope with suffering. It isn't as good at helping them to cope with affluence."

"Well, it's much easier to help people to cope with suffering. The affluent don't want to listen to you."

"This is true of Catholic communities?"

"I think I would have to say yes. But I'm not pessimistic about it when people will empty their pockets to help the starving in Ethiopia."

"How do you square that with what you've just said about 'numero uno'?"

"Or with the violence all over the globe? This is the big paradox."

"It seems that whereas people once gave to the church, they now give to Bob Geldof."

"Yes, but God is not a prisoner in a church building. You meet God in people. You meet God in suffering. God's giving out messages. Read the signs of the times. God is saying that the Kingdom of God is the one thing that counts. Now the church is the servant of the Kingdom, it's the place where you find Kingdom values most concentrated. But if people are contributing to Bob Geldof to feed the poor in Ethiopia, that's the Kingdom of God they're building up."

Tom Winning paused there, and said he wanted to fill in a missing piece. This whole idea of judgement — well, if there was a judgement, people's destiny would depend on how much compassionate love they had shown to their fellow men and women. Yes, that was the acid test.

"You say 'if'. But there is a day of judgement, isn't there? Isn't it called the great day?"

"I don't know what happens. He's not sitting there with a big book on His knees saying, 'Hey, you slipped up last Wednesday.' He's not catching us out. He's a loving God. We are our own judges."

"So what about this day of judgement?"

"It's probably a metaphor."

"Meaning?"

"There will be one. But we'll settle our own destiny."

"A lot of Christians" — I was thinking of one or two in this book — "find it difficult to accept the virgin birth as historical fact. Do you have any problem with it?"

"No, but there's a hierarchy of truths. I wouldn't say you would be a heretic if you didn't believe in it. If Christ is not God, I'm all washed up. But if Mary is not a virgin, there are lots of things that are still true."

"Well, let's look at the divinity of Christ. There are Christians who are even sceptical about the resurrection. Do you have any problem with that?"

"I believe it, so I have no problem."

"Bodily resurrection?"

"Aye, that He rose again and you're not going to find His body anywhere in Jerusalem. If resurrection means anything, it implies that there was this body brought back to life — but a new life, a different life. It's a body on a different level of being. An impassable body, not visible. But then He appeared before them in bodily form on occasions."

"Why did He do that?"

"As a concession to their faith. To build up their faith. But it wasn't that He got up and came out of the tomb and walked along to the next tomb and had breakfast. Not like that."

"It occurs to me that we haven't mentioned the Pope."

Archbishop Winning smiled broadly at my mention of this omission.

"He's a bit of a hard-liner, isn't he? On birth control, for example."

"Oh, he'll never give on that. His successor won't either. Or the guy after that."

"Why not? There are many Catholics who are deeply unhappy about the Church's teaching on this matter."

"I know, but they're living in a society which finds the teaching unhelpful and unfashionable."

"What precisely is it that society finds unhelpful and unfashionable?"

"That every act of intercourse has to be open to life."

"Is that teaching tenable any longer? If we go on procreating at the present pace, the planet will drive itself to destruction. There will be too many people."

"But you've got to allow for the restraints of human nature. And it's not every week in the month a woman is capable of bearing a child."

"That still leaves plenty of time to over-populate the planet."

"But think of the vast inequalities in the world. If the Africans and the Indians were getting a fair share of the world's goods there'd be nothing to worry about. But we've got two thirds of it, they've only got one third — and that's where the weans are. Responsible parenthood is what the Church preaches. We're not suggesting people proliferate like animals."

At which point in our interesting discussion, the Archbishop rose and ordered tea.

"You talked earlier about the goodwill of non-Catholics."

"Oh yes, I find a lot of goodwill and rapport with our separated brothers. More than I've ever found before."

"You've been to the General Assembly of the Church of Scotland. What did you make of that?"

"It's a pity it's only on for a week," he joked. At least I think — hope — he was joking. "I've got a great admiration for the Church of Scotland, but the General Assembly...well, it's very male-dominated, isn't it?"

"That's the pot calling the kettle black."

"Ah, but our structures are mixed. When we call a meeting of a diocesan assembly, it's men and women, clergy and lay people. And sometimes, I think the Assembly interferes too much in things that don't concern it..."

"You mean the Church and Nation Committee has ideas above its station?"

"A wee bit. Sometimes they presume a privileged place — would you like a cup? — something akin to the Catholic Church in Italy."

"Oh, really?"

As the Archbishop poured tea, he continued to poke a little harmless fun at the pretensions of the Presbyterian brethern.

"Yes, I always think of the Catholic Church in Italy and the Church of Scotland together. And the attendance is about the same, too. Take sugar?"

"But a lot of what you've been talking about in the last hour has been political. Aren't the churches entitled to speak out on political issues..?"

"Oh yes," he said, vigorously stirring his tea. "That's our job. To be prophetic. To proclaim what's happening. To denounce what's not. I'm not against that. I just think sometimes they're too openly political."

"What does an Archbishop do when he's not being an Archbishop? You list your recreation as watching football. Which team do you watch?"

"Usually two at a time!" he replied, now thoroughly enjoying himself. "Well, I've always been a Celtic fan. But I've got to withdraw a bit from that."

"Why?"

"I wouldn't want too high a profile. And I would never go to a Rangers-Celtic match. I couldn't go like this anyhow (in clerical garb), or I'd be in danger of my life." Was he serious? Or was it all part of the elaborate West of Scotland football joke?

"What would you do with a free night, say?"

He thought carefully about that. "What would I do?" he repeated. "Well, I might have a talk to prepare, or a sermon to think about."

"That's hardly a free night."

"Aye, but I'd be free to do it! Or I might go out. Where would I go? I don't socialise, really. Don't go to people's houses. I might just stay at home, and fritter the night away doing sweet damn all."

"That sounds pleasant enough."

As I rose to leave, Archbishop Winning said something that no one else said to me during my whirlwind tour of the great and the good. He said he hoped that he hadn't bored me. I was able to assure him, with absolute candour, that he hadn't bored me a bit.

Local Hero

SIR IAIN NOBLE

Only one of the 4,500 prominent people included in Who's Who in Scotland lists his address and recreations in Gaelic. Letters will almost certainly reach Sir Iain Noble at his home on Skye if correspondents take care to use the correct post code (IV43 8QR). Which leaves the problem of his recreations:

"deasbad, comhradh, orain is ceol le deagh chompanaich."

"Could you tell me in English what you're up to?"

"To say that I enjoy the Gaelic environment didn't feel right in English. So the best way was to be slightly more descriptive, but to write it down in Gaelic."

"What is the translation?"

"Stimulating debate and conversation, songs and music in good company."

Sir Iain has been doing plenty of that since he bought a 12,000-acre estate at Sleat, in the south of the island, 17 years ago. He has turned the stereotype of the absentee landlord on its head, poured a personal fortune into the development of a once dying community, and inspired a local revival of Gaelic language and culture. In the Highlands and Islands, where rich landed incomers generally get (and deserve) a bad name, he is one of the good guys.

"You're not a native Gaelic speaker. Who taught you?"

"The girls in the kitchen as much as anyone else. I picked it up by drip feed, really."

"They say it's difficult to learn."

"I'm convinced that's an excuse people use when they don't want to learn it. It is actually quite hard at the beginning, because the spelling system is quite different from English and the pronunciation can be a bit tough till you get used to it. But the language as such is no more difficult than any other."

"How often do you speak Gaelic?"

"Oh, a lot. There are many people I would never dream of speaking to in English."

When Sir Iain arrived in Sleat, he was faced by the familiar symptoms of island depopulation and decline. The primary school (with only 22 pupils) was threatened with closure, the population was ageing, and there were few if any local industries apart from the traditional crofting. The extent of the revival can be measured in statistics. The school roll is now 80 and rising; unemployment in the parish is down to four per cent (compared to 25 per cent in Skye and Lochalsh as a whole); a large number of the natives who have returned to live and work in the area are graduates. Sir Iain is modest about his own contribution; in conversation, he usually avoids using the first person singular when referring to what has been achieved at Sleat. The fact remains, however, that it is his money, energy, initiative and encouragement — most of all, perhaps, his faith — which has made much of it possible.

Not everything has worked. An early attempt to re-launch the local fishing industry foundered. A textile business ran for 12 years without ever making a profit. But a fish farm is slowly recovering after being stricken by disease; a connoisseur's brand of whisky has been successfully established; now there are plans for a food production company. And the Gaelic college and library which he helped set up by converting a group of derelict farm buildings has made an important and lasting contribution to the island's cultural heritage.

"Did you find initially that the local people were suspicious of you?"

"It would have been surprising if they weren't. A lot of people were convinced that oil must be in sight, or that I had some other ulterior motive for coming. Then when I tilted into Gaelic they thought I must be crackers. A few even felt threatened by the resurrection of Gaelic, because they'd been brought up on Skye and yet were not Gaelic speakers — were they to be regarded as second-class citizens? So, yes, a lot of vibrations in all directions."

"But you weren't discouraged?"

"I rather enjoyed throwing myself into the middle of the ring with the sort of brass neck of an incomer. I found there was a pent-up desire to do something, but with emigration and lack of confidence, people hadn't had the nerve to do it. It only took one person, and there was a great welling-up of support on all sides."

"You've put a lot of your own money into it?"

"Yes, I suppose I have committed quite a lot to it. It could easily have been invested infinitely better, but I don't regret it. It's been very exciting. I have always thought that if you could solve the problems of the West Highlands you would know how to solve the problems of Scotland — they're the same problems, just slightly larger in scale."

"Are they? What about the communications difficulties of industry in the Highlands?"

"Yes. But they're only a degree worse."

"Isn't there also the Highland temperament to bear in mind?"

"The Highland temperament is excellent."

"The Highlanders are said to be a lazy people."

"I've never found that. Interestingly, anywhere in the world where there's a dying language, the neighbours say the people are lazy and prone to drink. That's without exception as far as I know. You find it with the Irish, the Bretons, the Maoris, the Red Indians — the lot. It's a standard sociological response when a community loses confidence in the survival of its own identity. Equally, whenever a language is revived, the community has acquired so much self-confidence that its economic problems have disappeared like matchsticks. I've now reached the view that language can be used as an economic tool, and that a really healthy Gaelic revival will mean in the long run that the Highland Board won't be needed. The community will get its act together more easily without need of grants and subsidies."

I have never heard anyone talk more positively about this apparently lost cause, and Sir Iain Noble does so with some authority: he has matched words with deeds. Yet it would be hard to imagine an unlikelier champion of community development in the Highlands and Islands than this elegant, well-bred baronet with the cultured voice and impeccable manners of the Anglicised Scot.

★ ★ ★

"You were born abroad. How did that come about?"

"My father was with the Foreign Office, and travelled quite a bit. When I was four, we went off to Shanghai. Later he was No. 2 in Argentina, then Ambassador in Finland, Poland, Mexico and Holland. I went to school in China, Argentina and England."

"Where in England?"

"The notorious Eton."

"What's notorious about it?"

"You pay a helluva lot of money, meet a lot of people who come from a certain strata in society, get a bad education."

"Did you like your father?"

"Strange thing. I really had a double family. When my father was away, as often as not I spent holidays at home in Scotland with my uncle and aunt. In a sort of a way, I was partly fostered — had two sets of parents."

"So you didn't know your father very well?"

"I did, certainly. He was an amazing person. He had a computer mind, total recall of facts and figures. Very good grasp of politics — he could see strands developing and describe them in a way that almost left no room for argument. He didn't always get it right, but he had a good way of analysing it. He was actually rather proud of being a Scot, and always regarded Argyllshire as home. But he was very much in the old-fashioned British mould. I wasn't, quite."

"How?"

"From quite early on, I thought things had to be done in Scotland, that Scotland was a special case. I've always been in favour of a parliament here and am more convinced than ever that it's the natural thing to do."

"Your father wouldn't have agreed?"

"He would have disapproved strongly. He would have become angry if I'd even suggested it. His view was that we had all fought a war together, that we were British and couldn't break that kind of thing up, that he'd seen nationalism at work in various parts of the world and that it was always dangerous."

"What would you have replied?"

"Had I been willing to provoke his wrath, I would have argued strongly that it's just as practical for Scotland to be part of Europe — like Denmark or Luxembourg — and that it would actually increase the UK voice in Europe. It would probably be very positive for England too."

"So you'd go the whole hog — an independent Scotland?"

"I'd be perfectly relaxed if we did, but on the whole Scots are a bit too frightened of new concepts. I wish that we could see the potential."

Eton is an uncommon breeding ground for Scottish nationalists. "If I had children," — he is unmarried — "I would make a point of making sure they were educated in Scotland. I wouldn't put them through the system at Eton, because that fills them with propaganda to be non-Scots. If they survive that and return to Scotland, they're very lucky."

After Eton and his otherwise itinerant childhood, Iain Noble had a strong desire to put down roots. It was only when he drifted from Oxford to London that he came to realise that what he really wanted was to live and work in Scotland — even if, thanks to the conditioning of his education, it did seem "almost like going into the wilderness". What brought him back eventually was the offer of a job by the Scottish Council (Development and Industry) in Edinburgh.

"And was it like going into the wilderness?"

"No, but I was afraid it would be. I'm sure a lot of people are. It's the London mentality. You say to yourself, 'Is there anybody interesting who lives there?' Stupid arrogance!"

"You've been back for 25 years. How has Scotland changed in that time?"

"In 1964, emigration was very bad, the industrial giants were collapsing, and everybody was trying hard to fill the place with Americans. Now we're tantalisingly on the edge of breaking through — you feel the wagon's beginning to move, though it actually hasn't yet. Partly that's because senior members of the Scottish establishment have put a damper on specifically Scottish initiatives."

"Who are you blaming?"

"The commercial establishment. And the landowning establishment such as it is — which is not without influence in London. Generally, the so-called leaders of our society. Quite a lot of them were brought up in English schools and have been through the propaganda machine. And they don't want the ground rules changed."

As an executive with the Scottish Council, he observed one manifestation of the malaise: a spate of take-overs of long-established Scottish companies by southern predators. What was needed, he decided, was a locally-based merchant bank which would help to reverse this unhappy trend. He tried to interest the Scottish clearing banks, but without much success. At the critical moment, having more or less decided to "bloody well to do it myself", he found himself sitting beside the Edinburgh lawyer Angus Grossart on a bus returning from a dinner. Grossart asked him if he had any good ideas and he mentioned his plan for a Scottish merchant bank. Grossart was immediately interested, the two men met the following day, and Noble Grossart — one of the great financial success stories of post-war Scotland — was born.

"You didn't stay long..."

"Four years. I'd never really wanted to be a banker, to be honest, and I only did it because I felt there was a need for such a thing. As Noble Grossart had by that time become pretty professional, I reckoned they could get on perfectly well without me. And I'd always wanted to do something in the Highlands."

Now Sir Iain divides his life between his estate on Skye and a splendid office in Georgian Edinburgh, where he and two other Nobles run a small merchant bank of more recent origin. "I like to tell people that I spend half of my time in Edinburgh and two-thirds of it on Skye," he joked.

In the New Town drawing room where we met, the remains of a power breakfast lay on a boardroom table. In this incongruous setting, I found myself in the unusual situation of challenging a leading Scottish financier to tell me why his vision of an independent Scotland would work. What did he say, for example, to the argument that, as soon as customs barriers were erected at the border, the money would start flowing out of Scotland?

"The people who say that are looking for reasons to justify their pre-conceived notions. They're trying to scare-monger. Whether the money flows out or not would depend entirely on whether the new parliament had any credibility, whether it had good judgement or not."

"What would it have to do to make sure the money didn't flow out?"

"There is one very simple solution. The Scottish parliament

would only have to say, 'Our taxes in Scotland are going to be five or 10 per cent lower than England's', and the Treasury in Scotland would have its coffers filled. There would be a positive inflow of money if we got the taxes low enough."

"Are you talking about making Scotland a tax haven?"

"I'm not in favour of that approach, because it could lead to the wrong instincts and the wrong kind of people arriving. But if we had an attractive tax regime, we could begin to compete with places like Luxembourg, which is one of the most prosperous countries in Europe because of its tax rates — a place where people want to set up Euro businesses."

"What you're suggesting wouldn't do much to create jobs in manufacturing."

"That's quite true, but the financial sector is a big employer and has a lot of room for growth. Then we could say to ourselves: 'How can we create an industrial base? What sectors should we go for? Let's think it out carefully. Where do we want to be in 15 or 20 years' time? Let's work back from that.' Whereas on the whole people are living by pragmatism, fending off crises, occasionally having a brilliant new idea — but there isn't a long-term strategy."

"And that can't come unless there's a Scottish parliament?"

"I don't see any reason why we should expect Westminster to think in terms of a Scottish strategy. They don't want Scotland to be better off than the rest of the UK. But we have the team instinct. We would want to prove that we are indeed more innovative than the rest of the world — which we always were."

"Are there the people of stature in Scotland to bring it about?"

"I'm sure they're there, but maybe we don't have a way of creating them — or perhaps we've let too many leak out to Hong Kong. I attended Burns Night last year in Hong Kong. There were 450 people in the room, all in kilts, and the mood was electric. After the speeches, they passed around Scottish song books, and they simply shouted them out at the tops of their voices. Most of them were standing on their chairs singing them — and when they'd finished going through the book once, they went all the way through it again. As an expression of Scottish pride among exiles, it was very moving. And I thought to myself at the time, 'Dammit, why aren't these people in Scotland? An injection of 450 people of that calibre by itself would probably solve all our economic problems at once.' Let's have a crack at bringing them all back, before the Chinese get them!"

Sir Iain was getting quite carried away. I was getting quite carried away myself.

Gentleman George

GEORGE YOUNGER

It had been a disastrous day for the Scottish Tories. An opinion poll in the Glasgow Herald coinciding with the start of Mrs Thatcher's autumn visit north of the border put the party at 16 per cent in Scotland. Meanwhile, splashed across the front page of the Sun, there were embarrassing allegations about the private life of Professor Ross Harper, President of the Scottish Conservative and Unionist Association. (Before the week was out, he was Past President.)

When I reported to Ayr Racecourse for my late afternoon appointment with the former Secretary of State for Defence, Mrs Thatcher had evidently been and gone. Portraits of the lady were being dismantled in the foyer of the Eglinton Rooms and packed away in vans, the police and security men were looking a bit spare, and a Conservative official was telling topical jokes about slippers.

Presently, George Younger emerged with his wife Diana from an upstairs room and suggested that we go somewhere more congenial for our chat. A small fleet of cars — Mr and Mrs Younger and me in one, his security men in another, his constituency agent in a third — set off for afternoon tea at the Savoy Park Hotel.

We had just started the interview when a little old lady espied her local MP in a corner of the lounge, and came towards us with the quiet determination of Miss Marple in pursuit of the guilty party.

"Excuse me," she announced. "May I speak to Mr Younger?" The security men — ensconced over tea and scones in a far corner of the lounge — hardly stirred. Then came the words dreaded by all public figures: "You won't remember me..." Lo and behold, however, Mr Younger did — not only her name but a convincing detail about their last meeting umpteen years ago.

"Oh, we'll miss you, we'll miss you," she sighed. "I don't know what we're going to do without you."

Mr Younger gently put his arms around her. "Don't worry," he said, "you're stuck with me for a while yet. I won't be going until the next general election." Whereupon the little old lady, moderately reassured, tottered off.

It was only a month since the MP for Ayr had taken his constituents and the whole political world by surprise with his decision to resign his Cabinet post and become a banker. But perhaps it was not so surprising after all. Mr Younger will automatically become a member of the House of Lords upon the death of his father, Viscount Younger of Leckie, who is in his eighties; his Ayr seat is in any case among the most marginal in the country.

"What did Mrs Thatcher say when you told her?"

"She was pretty shocked. We had a fairly impressive fireworks display. But once I'd explained what I was doing and why, she came round to the idea and could understand it. As indeed did Willie Whitelaw, who was the only other person I consulted apart from Diana. To my surprise he said, 'Well, it may seem strange, but I think you're absolutely right. I ought to have left politics a bit earlier than I did.'"

"Have you had time to miss being a Cabinet minister?

"Oh, I find it very hard."

"What's hard about it?"

"It's just that after 10 years in the Cabinet, I felt part of the running of Britain. It's quite difficult to read the news and feel you're not part of it any longer."

"Are you starting to regret resigning?"

"I don't regret it at all. I came to a point earlier this year when I had to look at my life as a whole. I'm destined for the House of Lords anyway, and I don't find the prospect of being a minister in the Lords very attractive."

"Why not? Carrington was Foreign Secretary from the Lords."

"That's true, but I don't feel it's really at the centre of things and it's not at all well paid. So I could either carry on — which was enormously tempting — or take one last chance to do something quite different. It's stimulating at the age of 57 to be looking at something totally new."

If the end of George Younger's political career was fairly dramatic in its impact, so was the beginning. In 1963, he was fighting a by-election in Kinross and West Perth when, in his words, the Conservative Party conference in Blackpool "blew apart": Harold Macmillan resigned as Prime Minister and the Earl of Home became his unlikely successor. A seat in the Commons had to be found for Sir Alec; Kinross and West Perth happened to be available there and then.

"It was a lifetime's experience for me in a single week," Mr Younger remembered. "Suddenly my telephone became red hot, all sorts of people ringing up and asking me if I was going to give Alec Douglas-Home the seat. Well, it was clear to me that it was the natural thing to do. I then had to continue with the campaign on his behalf, with the world's press listening to every word I said as if I was a serious politician — whereas the fact was I knew nothing about nothing. I must say returning to work afterwards was an anti-climax."

"Would you have been happy to remain an industrialist — if a political career hadn't happened for you?"

"I'm sure I would have been happy, because I am normally happy doing whatever I'm doing. I was even happy joining the Army. You have to make the best of what comes up. But if I had never been in politics, I would have thought at some point: 'Why have I spent my whole life just making money or selling things? Why haven't I done something more meaningful — more central to the government of the country?'"

Mr Younger is from a Scottish brewing dynasty with a strong tradition of political involvement. His great grandfather also represented Ayr, and was a Conservative Chief Whip; his uncle Kenneth was a Labour MP for 15 years. But neither his father nor grandfather was active politically. Politics were not much talked about at home.

"So your father didn't influence you politically?"

"Not at all. But he did in lots of other ways. From him, I got a feeling of great dedication to duty. He's very strong on that."

"What does it mean, this sense of duty?"

"My family would describe it as an inability to turn down any invitation. Which I must confess is substantially true!"

"So how did you get interested in politics?"

"I was interested in political subjects at school (Winchester). I was just old enough to be aware of the 1945 election and was thrilled by the Labour victory. It sounded terrific to me. My mother was in tears about it and my father was looking pretty gloomy, but I couldn't understand why."

"When did you become a Tory?"

"During the most formative years — between 14 and 20. By the time I got to university, my views had changed. I identified with anything that was not socialism."

"And yet historians look kindly upon the Attlee administration. It's seen as a good, perhaps even a great government. A reforming government."

"I agree with that. It had a shot at doing what it set out to do, and there's no doubt we needed a change of course. But my opinions in 1950 reflected the general malaise everybody felt — shortages, rationing, that kind of thing."

"What does Conservatism mean to you?"

"Emotionally I identify with the carers. I want to sort out people's problems. That's a strong motivation with me — perhaps stronger than it is for some Conservatives. What makes me a very strong Conservative is that I'm absolutely convinced the socialist idea of running the economy doesn't produce the goods, doesn't motivate people. And it runs contrary to human nature."

"How does it?"

"Because human nature is to do things for other people now and then, when you've got time for it, when it suits you. It is not human nature to work flat out for other people all the time. But socialism requires you to do that — to think that it would be better if people generally were well off rather than you."

"You make socialism sound pretty noble."

"Admirable in many ways. But people aren't like that. The only thing that motivates people is working better and earning more and doing well for their families. The good people use the freedom that gives them to help others. That is Conservatism."

"Does Mrs Thatcher care about the poor? There's a widespread feeling that she doesn't."

"Yes, and for that to be the general view when we have done more for the poorly off than any previous government is really a most talented bit of non-achievement. It's remarkable how good we are at doing the right thing economically but how incredibly bad we are at presenting it."

"Oh, come. All the skills of the London advertising industry have been employed to present the Conservative government in a favourable light. And it's worked for you in three successive general elections..."

"But what we haven't succeeded in doing is getting the electorate to say, 'The Conservatives are really marvellous for the Health Service, they really care about it'."

"Maybe that's because you don't."

"We've done more for it than anyone else, and yet the general view is that we are against it."

"It comes back to Mrs Thatcher. Somehow she doesn't appear to be a caring person."

"She's actually a great softy when it comes to people."

"Individually, perhaps. But is she a great softy for the unemployed or the poor?"

Mr Younger repeated that it was a problem of communications, not substance, and that Mrs Thatcher had done the most incredibly kind things. I thought we should move on.

After gifting Kinross and West Perth to Sir Alec — a gesture which instantly made him a favourite son of the Conservative Party — George Younger did not have to wait long for another shot at Westminster. In 1964, the year that the Tories lost power nationally to Harold Wilson after 13 years of unbroken rule, he followed in his great-grandfather's footsteps as MP for Ayr.

"How does the Commons now compare with 1964? Is it a better place?"

"The standard of debating is much less good and the standard of behaviour is worse, though not worse than it's ever been — some of the things they said about Queen Victoria just wouldn't be acceptable today. But the conduct of members has deteriorated in the last 25 years, there's no doubt about that."

I wondered if that was a reflection of the increasing polarity between the two sides — the growing bitterness. Mr Younger thought not. He had a hunch that it simply mirrored a rougher edge in society generally. I suggested that still didn't explain the decline in the quality of the speaking. Were the wrong people going into politics?

"There's an element of that perhaps, but it's largely due to television. Before there was television, politicians had to prepare speeches. Now you pop along with your press release in your pocket and you respond to the thing that happened 10 minutes ago on the news. You're a sort of offshoot of Panorama, really."

"So ability on the box is an important quality in a modern politician?"

"That, and a general penchant for publicity."

"Are you sorry about it?"

"In a way. But that's probably a fault in me."

"What else do you need, apart from a penchant for publicity?"

Mr Younger put stamina top of the list. His great-grandfather, whose constituency included Prestwick, Troon, Inveraray and Campbeltown as well as Ayr, visited parts of his territory perhaps once a year, and that was perfectly acceptable in those days. Now an MP was expected to be at every whist drive.

"Do you complain about that?"

"I don't. But it is much more of a strain."

If I had to choose anyone to have a finger on the nuclear button, I might well choose gentleman George. I cannot imagine this thoroughly nice chap blowing us all to smithereens without a very good and pressing reason. I asked him whether, as Secretary of State for Defence, he literally did have his finger on the button. Of course, he wouldn't answer that one straight. Assuming for the sake of argument that it was at least fairly close, had the responsibility ever worried him?

"Not at all. I've always been conscious of the fact that I grew up during the war and that my parents and all around me were fighting for the existence of this country. We are only here — you and I are only talking here — because of that. I consider it essential for any free nation to be able to defend itself."

"Is there anything in politics you regret having done?"

"Oh, all sorts of little things. But I don't recall any major policy thing I got wrong, except one — I had quite a role in the Sixties in persuading Mr Heath to go for a Scottish Assembly. I do regret that."

"You can say that with the Tories standing at 16 per cent in the polls? Aren't you digging the most terrible hole for yourselves by refusing any form of devolution?"

"The poll is temporary, I wouldn't put too much on that. But I feel so strongly about this, actually, that I would really rather stick to what is so overwhelmingly right for Scotland and lose, than compromise."

"Even if you're increasingly isolated from other respectable opinion? I mean, what's wrong with devolution?"

"What's wrong is that it wouldn't work. It would be a recipe for conflict between Scotland and Westminster. And it would mean that we would quite quickly become irrelevant. Everyone would simply say, 'Thank God, the Scots have gone! Fine! Here's your share, get on with it, and shut up!'"

"A lot of Scots might buy that."

"But apart from a great deal of conflict and bitterness how would it end up? We would have no further effective role in Britain, and we would begin to get different standards in housing and health. It could only mean that England would dominate."

George Younger still carries at least one of the encumbrances of office: the security presence will be with him a while yet. And he is not quitting entirely, as he was at pains to make clear to me; some role in shaping the future of Conservatism in Scotland undoubtedly awaits him. Given his own and his party's inflexible position on Scottish home rule, it is difficult to see what that future might be. The unswerving support of little old ladies in the Savoy Park Hotel, Ayr, no longer seems enough.

Pass the Sick Bag, Alice

SIR JOHN JUNOR

My encounter with the Sage of Auchtermuchty was ill-starred from
the beginning. A few days before we were due to meet in his office
at Express Newspapers, Sir John Junor unexpectedly quit his
celebrated column after the new editor of the Sunday Express said
something which offended him. His secretary telephoned to ask if I
would mind going instead to Sir John's home in Surrey. Just when I
had reconciled myself to that, another message: the rendezvous
now was to be the Hilton International at Gatwick Airport.

As he strode into the lounge on the stroke of 11 a.m., the doyen
of Fleet Street looked like a man in a hurry. He was dressed for the
golf course. His shirt, tightly drawn over one of the best-known
bellies in British journalism, bore the insignia "Walton Heath". He
was taller than I expected; even at the age of 70, he must cut a
commanding figure on the 1st tee.

I led the way to a table in a quiet corner, but Sir John had other
ideas. "What's wrong with this?" he demanded in a Scottish rasp,
settling himself at the table of his choice.

"I'm golfing at Walton Heath," he announced. "You've got half
an hour."

"Let's see how it goes."

"You can see how it goes, but I'm off after half an hour."

Then matters took a sudden turn for the worse. Sir John has been
writing about Auchtermuchty for so long — holding it up as a
symbolic oasis of sanity in an otherwise fallen world — I had got
into my head that this was where he was born. He scoffed at this

absurd suggestion and said that I was alone in thinking such a thing. Hadn't I read the piece about him in the previous week's Sunday Times? He was not impressed to learn that I hadn't.

It transpired that he was a Glaswegian who had lived as a child "round about the Botanic Garden". "The west end?" "Well, Maryhill. That sort of area."

The connection with Auchtermuchty is, then, purely professional. In her recent autobiography the Daily Express columnist Jean Rook suggested that Junor — who she described as a "canny, not to say muck-mean Scot" — had invented Auchtermuchty: that the dour little Highland village was just a product of his imagination. Perhaps Ms Rook was nearer the truth than she knew.

"I was looking for a sort of Brigadoon for my column," Sir John explained. "A village which would contrast the old normality — decency, old-fashioned virtues — against the ugliness of the outside world. I wanted a place that had an attractive name. I thought of Ecclefechan, but finally decided on Auchtermuchty. It's got a tremendous guttural twist to it. It conjures up cobbled streets."

"Have you ever been in it?"

"Many times. It's on the way to St Andrews, where I play golf. So I'm a constant visitor. But anonymously, always."

"Did you find that it fulfilled your expectations?"

"Oh, yes. I think it is a place where time has stood still to a certain extent. There are many places like it throughout Europe. It's the capital cities and industrial towns which have really changed so drastically, don't you think?"

"What about Glasgow?"

"Glasgow I no longer know. I'm in and out of it before I know what's happened. I haven't been in the centre of Glasgow for years."

"Did you come from a prosperous background?"

"Oh God, no. Did you?"

"What sort of man was your father?"

"He was works manager of a steel works in Possilpark."

"Did you get on with him?"

"Yes, I got on with him."

"He was a Scot of the old school, perhaps?"

"Yes. Very orthodox in his views. I don't say I had a great

camaraderie with him."

"And your mother?"

"She was a very hard-working business lady, ambitious for her children, and sacrificed everything to get them a good education."

"What was the result of her sacrifice?"

"One son became a headmaster, one became a doctor. I'm the third."

"Were you a happy child?"

"Yes, I've been happy all my life. Glasgow University was great fun. Then came the Navy and that was great fun. The war was great fun. I've had a ball all the time."

He was speaking impatiently and edgily: I had still not been forgiven for the Auchtermuchty gaffe and for failing to buy the Sunday Times. Now that he had disposed of the first 20 years of his life in a few reluctant monosyllables, I asked him how he had entered journalism. For once, he gave me a fairly detailed answer. He had been a pilot in the second world war. The Admiralty had struck on the idea of launching a magazine for the Fleet Air Arm, and asked him to help A.P. Herbert to edit it. In the event, Herbert didn't want the job and he was appointed instead — "that got me launched."

"Had you wanted to be a journalist before this?"

"Yes, but I'd really wanted to be a politician. I looked upon journalism as a route to that."

"Were politics discussed in your family?"

"Not at all. But I became interested when I was at university. I'd been in that Munich period, and had reacted strongly against the Chamberlain government and the appeasement policy."

He stood three times as a Liberal candidate. The first time, he came within 612 votes of winning; the third time, he polled the highest Liberal vote in the UK but still lost (in Dundee West). But he was now a rising star within the Beaverbrook newspaper empire, and faced a choice.

"When I got back to London, Lord Beaverbrook took me aside and said, 'What's it going to be? Politics or journalism? If you make it journalism, I'll put the golden crown of journalism on your head.' I made it journalism."

"Are you sorry you didn't choose politics?"

"Not really. I became very friendly with many politicians of all parties, and one was aware that they were always kept on a leash by their constituencies — terrified to say or do anything in case they offended them. And power was so transitory. In government, they'd have their chauffeurs waiting outside the front door of the restaurant, then came the election and they were out looking for a taxi or more often a bus. They never made any money anyway."

"Would you have been a good MP?"

"I think so, yes."

"Why? You're not a man who likes to be kept on a leash, are you?"

"No, but then I wouldn't have been kept on a leash. I'd have got to the top in politics, as I did in journalism. If you work hard and apply yourself, you get to the top in anything."

"Are there politicians you admire?"

"Good God, yes. Margaret Thatcher for one. Harold Wilson I admired."

"They're two very different sorts of politicians. One was a pragmatist, the other a...."

I was going to say "conviction politician". But Sir John interrupted with a more extravagant description of the Prime Minister:

"A revolutionary. A radical revolutionary."

"Poles apart from Wilson, certainly."

"I like all politicians," said Sir John, who was obviously not interested in pursuing the distinction. "I think most of them are pretty honest. I find myself at home with them."

"More so than with journalists?"

"Journalists and politicians belong to the same breed. We're all part of serving the public, aren't we? When a man becomes a politician, unless he's a tenth-rate politician, he thinks he can do some good. And when a chap becomes a journalist, he wants to do some good too." The way Sir John spoke, it was almost as if naked ambition and lust for power were concepts alien to this noble race.

The "golden crown" bestowed by Lord Beaverbrook was the editorship of the Sunday Express. Junor was appointed in 1954, at the age of 35, and retired in 1986 — a reign of impressive longevity in an organisation famed for brutal dismissals.

"How did you get on with Beaverbrook?"

"It was a sort of love-hate relationship. We respected each other. At one stage, I quit — I was within a week of leaving the job at the time of the Profumo affair because I felt I could no longer support

Harold Macmillan as Prime Minister. Of course, the Sunday Express and Lord Beaverbrook were committed to supporting the Tory government. So I submitted my resignation, and was working out my contract when I heard on the radio that the Prime Minister had gone into hospital. I knew that was the end of Macmillan, and that I was saved. I carried on after that for another 20 years."

"Do you have any regrets about staying in the job as long as you did?"

Sir John had been unwinding a little, but I discovered that he could be mellow only in short bursts. It was time for another exocet from highest Auchtermuchty:

"I've no regrets about anything! What the hell's the point in having regrets in life? It's done! I've had fun!"

"Has journalism changed much since you became an editor?"

"In one way it has. Beaverbrook used to take us walking through the park. Not just me, but his other young men. Every morning, he went for an hour's walk and he would have someone with him. He used to give us marvellous ideas, but he also used to lecture us on journalistic ethics. His first adage was, 'Never put the police on anyone.' That is, don't try and act as narks and informers. That doesn't mean he was against investigative journalism, just that you shouldn't go out of your way to expose some minor wrongdoing. The second and more important point was, 'Always remember, fucking is free.' You must never, ever, expose infidelity. If a man is having an affair, you don't write about it in a newspaper in such a way as to break up his marriage."

"That rule hasn't been observed much in recent years."

"And that's rather sad, because so many marriages have broken up which needn't have broken up, simply because of exposure in newspapers."

"You think that's one of the bad things about the tabloid press?"

"A pity, yes. A pity there's so much intrusion. And yet, one wouldn't want a press that didn't investigate and expose hypocrisy. If you get a politician who loves seeing his picture in the paper kissing babies at garden parties, I don't see why he should recoil if the baby turns out to be 19 and in a night club."

"When did you start writing the column?"

"I only wrote the column because someone had to take John Gordon's place. He had been editor of the Sunday Express, and writing this very good column which was terribly important to the newspaper. As he became older and less fit, I constantly worried what was going to happen when he finally toppled off the perch. He was about 83 before he did. In his last year, he was clearly not absolutely on the ball. What I used to do was to write a series of memos to him, which were in effect the paragraphs of his column. He accepted that pretty gratefully. Once he died, I wrote the column for a while with just the initials J.J. at the bottom. Then one day I thought what the hell — and put my name up at the top." And at the top it remained, until a few days before our meeting.

I reminded Sir John that in a graceful tribute in Sunday's Observer — which I had read in preference to the Sunday Times — Richard Ingrams had mentioned J.J.'s habit of sailing pretty close to the wind. Did he agree?

"Absolutely. That's the whole purpose of a column."

"Is it?"

"Sure. Because you want to tell the truth about people and our libel laws are sometimes a little bit intimidating. So if you can find a way of exposing villainy without actually getting yourself into a libel case — you do it."

"Are there any targets you particularly like attacking?"

"Just hypocrisy."

"What kind?"

"Any kind."

"Give me an example."

"That's terribly difficult off the top of one's head. Once I've written my columns, I forget what's in them."

"Does it worry you that your acerbic wit hurts people?"

"Everything hurts people. You can't report a murder trial without hurting someone. Just think what the children of the man on trial feel. All news hurts."

"So there's nothing you've written about someone that you've later regretted?"

"No."

"Private Eye paid you the great compliment of doing a pastiche of your column."

"I enjoyed that enormously."

"It was a pretty good imitation, wasn't it?"

"If you think so. It's not for me to say."

The two phrases which Private Eye picked up — they have entered the language of satire — were 'I think we should be told' and 'Pass the sick bag, Alice'. When I asked him about their origins, Sir John got irritated again. I should have read the Sunday Times. I shouldn't stick to one Sunday newspaper. It really wasn't good research. Then he answered the question.

"'I think we should be told' I only wrote once to the best of my memory. 'Pass the sick bag, Alice' I only wrote once. But they were taken up in the pastiche, and repeated time and time again."

"You really never used them again?"

"No. Why should one? Do you write the same thing again and again?"

I had to confess to Sir John that it had been known.

Fearful that my alloted half-hour was evaporating fast, I turned the conversation sharply to thoughts of Scotland. Since the Sage of Auchtermuchty was such an admirer of Mrs Thatcher, I wondered why other Scots loathed her so heartily.

"I don't know whether you're correct in saying that the Scots loathe her."

"The Tories are 16% in the polls in Scotland. Doesn't suggest they love her, does it?"

"I am unaware of these polls," he said darkly. "But if there is a dislike of Mrs Thatcher among the Scots, it's for two or three reasons. One is that the Scots are a male chauvinist race, and not any longer particularly intelligent, because most of the best people have left Scotland. They are also a whingeing people, which they never used to be. They have made a mess of industry. They've buggered up shipbuilding, they've buggered up the motor car industry. When the government tried to put car factories into Bathgate, the Scots workers were the worst in Britain. They wouldn't work if it was raining, or if it was too hot, so the car factories folded up."

The Sage paused before resuming his abusive rant.

"What else did they bugger up?" he asked rhetorically. "Just about everything! They resent the English, they resent especially a woman telling them what to do!"

"Maybe they resent the English because they have a frustrated sense of nationhood."

"Sense of nationhood! What sort of nationhood is being

frustrated? Lord Beaverbrook set up the Scottish Daily Express, and did so not only to make money but because he cared about Scotland, he looked upon himself as Scots. But in the end the Scottish Daily Express was killed by the Scottish workers. They treated us in the most terrible fashion. They started censoring the newspaper — they wouldn't print it if it had a cartoon in it they didn't like."

"It was as bad in Fleet Street if not worse."

"Nothing of the kind! The Scots nowadays...and I'm so proud to be Scots...but nowadays you're a bunch of whingeing third-raters. Margaret Thatcher's too damned good for you all. And you resent her because she's got this upper class or simulated upper class Edinburgh accent. And you resent also the fact that she's pulling you out of the shit that you've put yourself into over so many years."

"Or because we feel she hasn't done nearly enough for Scotland."

"Balls! There's more money spent on Scotland than on anywhere else."

I started to laugh. Sir John laughed, too, the familiar stage scowl relaxing for a moment.

"You're a fine one to talk about the Scots. You got out."

"Yes, and pretty despondent I am when I look at those who remain."

Sir John glanced at his watch. The 1st tee at Walton Heath beckoned. I imagined him smashing a mighty slice into deep rough — unkindly hoped for it, if the truth be known.

"Have you ever felt inclined to return to Scotland? To stay, I mean?"

"Oh yes. It's like the salmon going back. In my mind, Scotland is my home. I remember a taxi driver in Edinburgh who was taking me to the station. I asked him if he'd ever been abroad. He had — as a matter of fact he'd been a prisoner of war. When the train on which he and his friends were travelling crossed the border into Scotland on their way home, they all got out at the first station and kissed the ground. Only yesterday, my daughter was saying how much she longed to go back and live in Scotland. Just a pity you're such whingers."

"Why didn't you go back if you like the place so much?"

"Because my job was here, and Scots trade unionists had killed Scottish journalism. I'll be leaving you, Kenneth, pretty soon."

"Who are the figures in Scottish history that interest you?"

"I suppose Mary Queen of Scots and John Knox."

"Why John Knox?"

"Because I'm a Calvinist, that's all."

"What does Calvinism mean to you?"

"It doesn't mean anything more than having a certain respect for morality as practised by others."

"What about belief?"

"Oh, I believe in God certainly. I'm not sure if I believe in anything else. How are you getting back?"

By an Air UK flight to Glasgow, as it happened. Unlike the taxi driver, I didn't kiss the ground on my arrival; nor did I hug the nearest whinger. After half an hour in the company of the Sage of Auchtermuchty, I was just glad to be home.